MINNESOTA

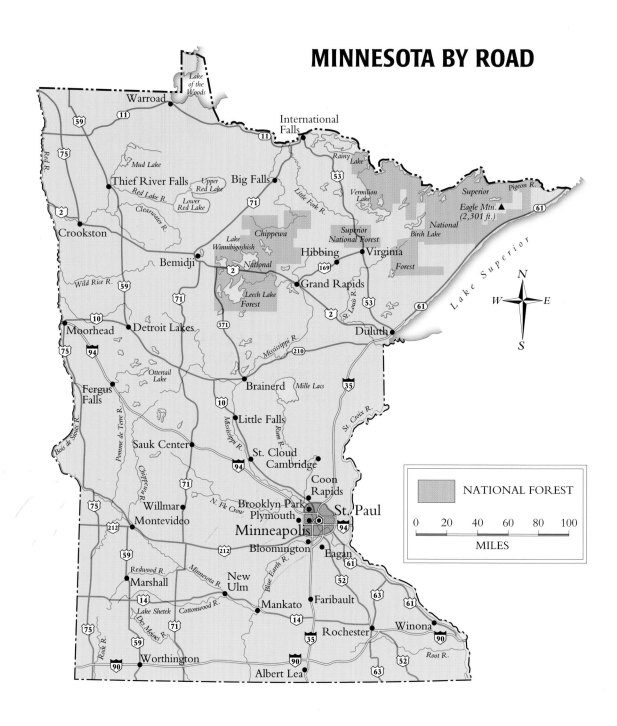

MINNESOTA BY ROAD

Lake of the Woods

Warroad

International Falls

Mud Lake

Thief River Falls

Upper Red Lake

Big Falls

Rainy Lake

Vermilion Lake

Superior

Eagle Mtn. ▲ (2,301 ft.)

Pigeon R.

Red Lake R.

Lower Red Lake

Little Fork R.

Crookston

Clearwater R.

Chippewa

Lake Winnibigoshish

National

Superior National Forest

National

Birch Lake

Bemidji

Hibbing

Virginia

Forest

Wild Rice R.

Grand Rapids

St. Louis R.

Lake Superior

Leech Lake Forest

Moorhead

Detroit Lakes

Duluth

Ottertail Lake

Mississippi R.

Fergus Falls

Brainerd

Mille Lacs

Pomme de Terre R.

Little Falls

Rum R.

St. Croix R.

Bois de Sioux R.

Sauk Center

St. Cloud

Cambridge

Chippewa R.

Coon Rapids

Willmar

N. Fk Crow

Brooklyn Park

Plymouth

St. Paul

Montevideo

Minneapolis

Bloomington

Eagan

Redwood R.

Minnesota R.

New Ulm

Blue Earth R.

Marshall

Lake Shetek

Cottonwood R.

Mankato

Faribault

Des Moines R.

Rochester

Winona

Rock R.

Worthington

Albert Lea

Root R.

N
W E
S

NATIONAL FOREST

0 20 40 60 80 100

MILES

CELEBRATE THE STATES
MINNESOTA

Martin Schwabacher

BENCHMARK BOOKS

MARSHALL CAVENDISH
NEW YORK

For my parents, Bill and Heidi Schwabacher

Benchmark Books
Marshall Cavendish Corporation
99 White Plains Road
Tarrytown, New York 10591-9001

Library of Congress Cataloging-in-Publication Data
Schwabacher, Martin.
Minnesota / Martin Schwabacher.
p.   cm. — (Celebrate the states)
Includes index.
Summary: Discusses the geographic features, history, government, people,
and attractions of the state known as the Land of Ten Thousand Lakes.
ISBN 0-7614-0658-1 (lib. bdg.)
1. Minnesota—Juvenile literature. [1. Minnesota.] I. Title. II. Series.
F606.3.S39   1999   977.6—dc21   98-39891   CIP   AC

Maps and graphics supplied by Oxford Cartographers, Oxford, England

Photo research by Candlepants Incorporated

Cover photo: Layne Kennedy

The photographs in this book are used by permission and through the courtesy of: *Greg Ryan/ Sally Beyer*: 6-7,
17, 18, 48-49, 58, 60, 62, 64-65, 73, 77(right), 80-81, 99, 100, 101, 106, 107, 109, 117(top), 136. *Layne
Kennedy*: 10-11, 14, 21, 53, 57, 61, 67, 75, 76(left), 76-77, 96-97, 115, 126, back cover. *The Image Bank*:
Burton McNeely, 13. *Minnesota Office of Tourism*: 15, 25, 72, 111, 113, 117(bottom). *Photo Researchers, Inc.*:
Tom & Pat Leeson, 23(top); Tim Davis, 23(bottom); Shambroom, 70, 123; Francois Gohier, 120.
The Minneapolis Institute of Art: 26-27, 31, 43. *W. Duncan MacMillan*: 29. *Brown County Historical Society*: 36.
Minnesota Historical Society: 40, 41, 44, 46, 103. *State Court Administration, MN Judicial Center*: 52. *Corbis
Bettmann*: 83, 84, 130(left). *Amalie Rothschild/Corbis-Bettmann*: 89. *UPI/Corbis-Bettmann*: 92, 128, 133.
Reuters/Corbis-Bettmann: 93, 131. *Joh Springer/Corbis-Bettmann*: 130(right). *George Rinhart/Corbis-Bettmann*:
132. *Archive Photos/American Stock*: 86. *Archive Photos/Press Association*: 90. *Archive Photos/Reuters/Brad
Rickerby*: 134. *Office of the Mayor of Minneapolis*: 94. *Gjert of Norway*: 110. *Office of the Secretary of State of
Minnesota*: 116. *Supreme Court Historical Society*: 129.

Printed in Italy

3   5   6   4

CONTENTS

MINNESOTA IS . . .

Minnesota is a land of lakes . . .

"I love living at the lake. It's my dream. I never want to sell this place."   —Arlene Daniel, Cedar Lake

"Our grandchildren constantly talk about going to the lake. This is the highlight of their summer."   —Katie Steffel, St. Paul

. . . cold winters . . .

"You've heard of winter wonderland? This is it—all the way into March."

—Merrill "Dutch" Cragun, Cragun's Resort near Brainerd

. . . and beautiful, unspoiled wilderness.

"Come, point your car to Minnesota's cool North woods. Let the tall pines be your roof, the stars your night-lamp, the spicy air your tonic!"   —Minnesota Tourist Bureau, 1935

Minnesota is a land of progressive politics . . .

"This city of lutefisk and liberals has long boasted a tradition of generous social programs and enlightened views on American race relations."   —Journalist Dirk Johnson

. . . small-town pride . . .

"Welcome to Northfield, home of cows, colleges, and content-ment."   —Roadside sign

. . . and polite people.

Minnesotans have "a sweetness of character that perhaps is brought out by bitter weather and sensory deprivation. . . . This is a state of people not so far removed from the farm, and farming is a civil business that believes in sharing new information and helping your neighbor. It produces good-hearted people who are tolerant, helpful and friendly."   —Writer Garrison Keillor

---

Minnesota is a land of bountiful farms, shady forests, rippling lakes, powdery snow, and polite, wholesome people. Minnesotans take good care of their state and each other, maintaining some of the best parks, schools, and government services in the nation. They have a wealth of opportunities to enjoy the outdoors, and they make the most of them, summer or winter.

Newsweek magazine once showed Minnesota's governor on the cover. He was standing in front of a sky-blue lake, wearing a plaid shirt, holding a big fish, and grinning. The picture was titled "The Good Life in Minnesota," and for many Minnesotans, that's just how life is.

1 THE NORTH STAR STATE

Minnesota's rich farmland and thriving Twin Cities of Minneapolis and St. Paul make it a great place to earn a living. But with miles of cool forests and sparkling lakes, it's an even better place to relax. More often than not, on a summer weekend, a real Minnesotan will be out fishing. "It's hard not to when you're right there on the lake, you know," says Deer River resident Ken Baldwin. "It's a big pastime around here."

SKY-BLUE WATERS

Minnesota is known as the Land of 10,000 Lakes, and this is no exaggeration. In fact, Minnesota has nearly 12,000 lakes of at least ten acres, and if smaller ones are counted, the number soars past 15,000. The state has so many lakes that some ended up with the same name. Minnesota has 201 Mud Lakes, 154 Long Lakes, and 123 Rice Lakes. Sixty-five towns in Minnesota have the word *lake* in their name, not counting words that mean lake or water in Native American languages. *Minnesota* itself means "sky-tinted water" in the Dakota language.

Most of Minnesota's lakes were formed thousands of years ago when giant sheets of ice called glaciers inched their way down from the frozen north. These glaciers—some more than a mile thick— gouged deep into the earth, scraping off the soil down to the bare

People come from all over to fish in Minnesota's lakes. Two million fishing licenses are sold each year in a state of fewer than five million people.

bedrock. By the time the glaciers retreated, they had transformed northern Minnesota into a rough, rocky landscape. Melting ice filled in the low spots, creating lakes.

Minnesota's northeastern corner is a triangle shaped like an arrowhead, with the beautiful, rugged north shore of Lake Superior on one side and the Canadian border on the other. The Arrowhead region in between contains thousands of small lakes. In the tranquil Boundary Waters Canoe Area Wilderness, you can canoe for

One young visitor to the Boundary Waters Canoe Area Wilderness recalled,
"It's fun. You can look up and there's the sky and the clouds. The woods are on
all sides. It's hard to describe. It's just like . . . free. Totally away from it all."

days without seeing another human being or hearing the sound of
a motor. Vacationers like Tim Starr come to enjoy "the complete
stillness, where the flat water reflects everything you see."

Early fur traders used to canoe from lake to lake, following rivers or
simply carrying their canoes overland to the next lake. The route
traced by these hearty travelers from Lake Superior to Lake of the
Woods forms part of the state's northern boundary. An odd chunk of
land on the northwestern side of Lake of the Woods was included

in the United States. This section of Minnesota, which cannot be reached by land without leaving the United States, pokes farther north than any other part of the country except Alaska—one reason Minnesota is called the North Star State.

In western Minnesota, the glaciers had a very different effect. There, when the ice melted, the water created a vast inland sea called Lake Agassiz. This lake existed for thousands of years and was the largest lake in the continent. Over the years, mud and silt settled on the lake bottom. When the giant lake finally drained, it left behind some of the flattest, richest farmland in North America. This area is called the Red River valley. The wide, flat valley barely rises

The fertile Red River valley produces many crops, including sunflowers. Minnesota ranks third in the nation in sunflower production.

at all for miles on either side of the Red River, making floods particularly devastating. Locals successfully fought off floodwater many times over the years, but in 1997, they were hit by the worst flood they had ever seen. "You just can't imagine fifty miles of water around you in every direction," said Jack Thompson of Breckenridge. Wendy Pearson of the National Weather Service said, "You've got to have a lot of respect for the water. What it can do is awesome."

A wide swath of lakes curves up the middle of Minnesota. These lakes formed between the mounds of dirt and crushed rock left behind by the glaciers. This lake region marks the edge of the Great Plains, which sweep uninterrupted over the bottom of the state. Once, rippling grassland stretched as far as the eye could see. In the 1800s, painter George Catlin said that the horizon formed "a perfect straight line around us, like that of the blue and boundless ocean." Today, the prairie has been fenced off into neat farms. A layer of rich topsoil that was pushed ahead of the glaciers as they surged south gave southern Minnesota some of the country's most fertile farmland.

The southeastern tip of Minnesota is the only part of the state the glaciers did not reach. According to writer D. J. Tice, "the southeast is a lakeless land of cold, rushing streams, high ridges, plunging ravines, and green-brown valleys rolling lazily into the distance, soft and lumpy as featherbeds." Though this area has almost no lakes, it's still a great place to fish, with some of the best fly-fishing streams anywhere.

Minnesota has 15,000 miles of rivers, including the Red River of the North and the Bois de Sioux, which form parts of the state's

IN LOVE WITH THE PRAIRIE

A vast sea of grass once covered much of the United States, including a third of Minnesota. The endless prairie awed early settlers, who felt tiny amid the shoulder-high grasses. Wild prairies contained hundreds of kinds of plants. Today, most prairies have been replaced by farms, where just a few plants are grown at a time.

A growing number of people have fallen in love with the rich but subtle variety of a truly wild prairie. Steve Henke and Nancy Peltola, who own land in southern Minnesota, trade seeds with other prairie lovers to recreate the variety of plants that once grew wild. Wandering through their little patch of prairie, Steve points out his new friends. "This is pussy toes . . . buffalo pea . . . harebell . . . wild rose. . . . Here's one of my favorites, prairie smoke. It looks like a puff of smoke."

A true prairie must burn now and then to keep other plants from moving in. Plains Indians used to set fires regularly to chase game, renew pastures, and drive off insects. Steve and Nancy carefully burned twelve acres of their prairie to help restore it to the way it once was. "Two weeks later," Steve said, "you couldn't tell it had ever been burned."

western border, and the St. Croix and Mississippi, which form parts of the eastern border. The Minnesota River joins the Mississippi at St. Paul, the state capital. The mighty Mississippi, the nation's most important river, starts in northern Minnesota as a tiny stream trickling out of Lake Itasca.

COLD—AND HOT

Minnesota is famous for frigid weather, and deservedly so. The cold winters force Minnesotans to put on so much clothing they some-

At the source of the mighty Mississippi in Itasca State Park, the river is so tiny that a child can crawl across it.

LAND AND WATER

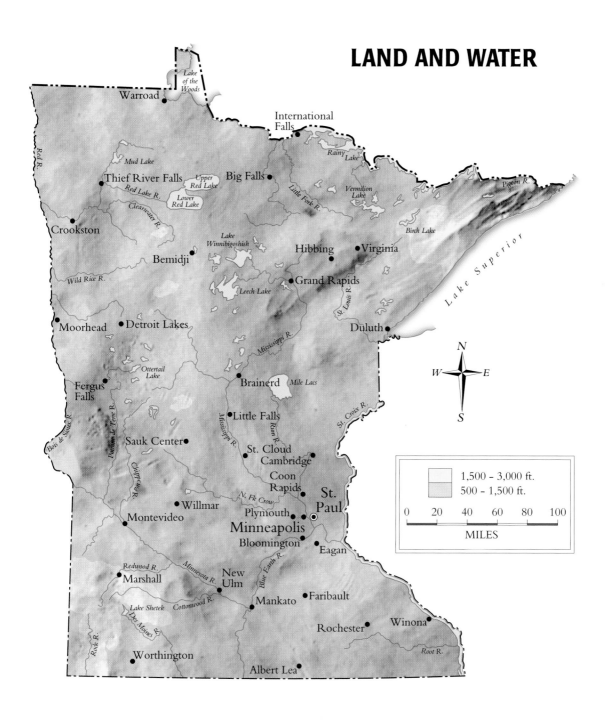

Lake of the Woods

Warroad

International Falls

Red R.

Rainy Lake

Pigeon R.

Mud Lake

Thief River Falls

Upper Red Lake

Big Falls

Little Fork R.

Vermilion Lake

Red Lake R.

Lower Red Lake

Clearwater R.

Lake Winnibigoshish

Birch Lake

Crookston

Bemidji

Hibbing

Virginia

Wild Rice R.

Grand Rapids

Leech Lake

St. Louis R.

Lake Superior

Moorhead

Detroit Lakes

Duluth

Mississippi R.

Ottertail Lake

Fergus Falls

Brainerd

Mile Lacs

N

W   E

S

Pomme de Terre R.

Little Falls

Bois de Sioux R.

Mississippi R.

St. Croix R.

Sauk Center

St. Cloud

Rum R.

Chippewa R.

Cambridge

Coon Rapids

N. Fk. Crow

St. Paul

Willmar

Plymouth

| | 1,500 – 3,000 ft. |
| | 500 – 1,500 ft. |

Montevideo

Minneapolis

Bloomington

Eagan

0   20   40   60   80   100

MILES

Redwood R.

Minnesota R.

New Ulm

Blue Earth R.

Marshall

Mankato

Faribault

Lake Shetek

Cottonwood R.

Des Moines R.

Rochester

Winona

Rock R.

Worthington

Root R.

Albert Lea

times look like puffy marshmallows. The temperature falls below zero degrees Fahrenheit an average of thirty-four days each year in the Twin Cities, and sixty-eight days in International Falls, way up north near the Canadian border. International Falls often records the coldest temperature anywhere in the lower forty-eight states—it's not uncommon to see the thermometer dip to forty below zero there. During a record cold snap in 1996, when one town reached sixty below, every school in the state had to be closed. Governor Arne Carlson explained, "I don't want an eight-year-old girl standing on the corner waiting in this kind of weather for a bus that will never come."

Except for the very coldest times, however, kids have a great time in the snow. They go sledding, build snowmen and forts, and have snowball fights. "I love Minnesota winters," says Minnesota native Dan Barton. "Everything is clean. Powdery snow is everywhere—the world is new. The entire neighborhood turns into a playground."

Of course, winter in Minnesota is not all fun and games. Darkness comes early in winter, and for some people, it's just too cold to go outside if they can help it. "When it gets to be six to nine months, it gets to be a lot," one Minnesotan admitted. "You go to school or work in the morning, it's dark and cold. You get out in the evening, it's dark and cold. You get cabin fever."

While Minnesota's winters are famous, fewer people know that Minnesota summers can also be uncomfortable. There are many lovely days, but July and August can be hot and muggy, with temperatures occasionally breaking one hundred degrees. And Minnesota's abundant water creates a perfect breeding ground for

A boy eats snowflakes during a Minnesota snowstorm.

mosquitoes. In remote areas, campers wear nets to protect them-selves from swarming insects. Ken Baldwin, who lives in a swampy, wooded area in central Minnesota, says he has to brush himself off thirty feet from his house, then run to the door so he doesn't bring a cloud of mosquitoes inside with him. "When the sun's out and there's a little bit of a breeze, it doesn't bother me. But when it's dark in the woods, it can get pretty bad," he says.

WILD THINGS

Though much of Minnesota is farmland, a third of the state is covered with trees. The north woods are filled with pine, fir, aspen, and
birch. Patches of maple, elm, and oak are sprinkled farther south.
Wild blueberries and raspberries offer tasty snacks to wandering
hikers, and wild roses, violets, asters, and goldenrod provide a feast
for the eyes.

The state's woods, fields, rivers, and lakes are full of wildlife.
Bears, skunks, raccoons, beavers, muskrats, and foxes are abundant. Lucky hikers may also spot moose, gray wolves, and eagles.
Minnesota's state bird, the common loon, can often be seen on
northern lakes. A black-and-white bird noted for its red eyes and a
white necklace, the loon is much loved for its distinctive call, which
sounds like eerie, ghostly laughter.

Many Minnesotans enjoy hunting and fishing. The state is home
to twenty-five kinds of ducks and several types of geese. Partridge,
sharp-tailed grouse, and ring-necked pheasant abound, as do
white-tailed deer. Popular game fish include northern pike, large-
mouth bass, brook trout, and walleye.

People are not the only creatures that stalk deer and other
animals. Human hunters share the north woods with about two
thousand gray wolves. Minnesota is the only state besides Alaska in
which wild wolves were never completely wiped out. Although
wolves do not attack people, their howls once sent shivers up the
spines of pioneer families, and they were hunted to near extinction.
In 1974, wolves were protected under the Endangered Species Act.
Although farmers used to insist on killing wolves, today, if a wolf

Although awkward on land, loons are terrific divers and swimmers. The sound of their eerie calls wafting across the rippling water of a remote lake is one of Minnesota's true delights.

Gray wolves were once hunted to near extinction. But after they were protected, they made a tremendous comeback and now range freely across the state.

kills a cow, the state compensates the farmer and removes the wolves. Bill Berg of the Minnesota Department of Natural Resources says, "People have come to accept the wolf as a critter they can live with." The efforts to save the wolf have been so successful that wolves now roam over almost half the state.

LISTENING TO THE WILDERNESS

Minnesotans love the outdoors, but sometimes they disagree over how best to enjoy their state's natural beauty. One argument arose over the use of Jet Skis, which allow people to zoom around on the water just as they do on snowmobiles onshore. Though Jet Skis are exciting to ride, they can be a nuisance. Instead of listening to the gentle lapping of the waves, everyone at the lake must listen to the constant buzzing of a motor. "People are saying, 'Give us some relief,'" said state representative Kris Hasskamp. "We're asking for four hours in a day to have some peace to listen to the loons." Many people wanted to ban the machines completely from smaller lakes, while others fought any restrictions. In 1997, the state legislature passed a law that limited the use of Jet Skis to day-time hours, from 9:30 A.M. to one hour before sunset, allowing everyone to enjoy the setting sun in silence.

Disputes also arise over the use of snowmobiles. The pristine Boundary Waters Canoe Wilderness Area bans them, but Voyageurs National Park allows them in certain areas. Some argue that with thousands of miles of snowmobile trails elsewhere in the state, parks such as Voyageurs should be left in serene, natural silence. Others contend that snowmobiles allow people to go places in winter they could not reach otherwise. David Dill, a frequent visitor to Voyageurs, respects both views. "When I take people snowmobiling here, I just love to stop and turn the lights off. Their eyes start to adjust, and they say, 'Oh my God!' and they see the sky is just a mass of stars. And the wolves start calling, and it's just this incredible environmental experience."

Snowmobiles were invented in Minnesota, and they remain a popular way to travel across snow-covered regions.

2 YESTERDAY AND TOMORROW

St. Anthony Falls about 1848, by Henry Lewis

Ten thousand years ago, when the last glaciers in what is now Minnesota were melting, huge animals roamed the earth. People known as Paleo-Indians hunted mammoths (which were like elephants, only bigger) and giant bison twice the size of today's buffalo. As the land grew warmer, there were berries and nuts to pick and rabbits and fish to catch.

EARLY MINNESOTANS

Around five thousand years ago, people living near Lake Superior found chunks of copper that they pounded into knives and spear-points. These were the first people in America to make metal tools. Later, people began gathering wild rice and planting corn, beans, and squash. By one thousand years ago, people in what is now southern Minnesota lived in towns, hunted with bows and arrows, caught fish with hooks and lines, and made beautifully decorated clay pots.

In the 1500s, the Dakota Indians lived in present-day Minnesota. They moved from place to place, following the cycle of the seasons. In the spring, they collected sap from maple trees to make sugar. They also fished, hunted ducks and geese, and caught muskrats and beavers for their warm fur. When the weather grew warmer, they planted corn and other vegetables. During the summer, the Dakota lived in large

American Indians gather wild rice by bending the stalks over their canoes and knocking the grains off with a stick. What falls in their canoes, they keep; the grains that land in the water become the seeds for next year's plants.

wooden buildings that housed two or three families. The women collected berries and roots, and the men hunted buffalo. As summer ended, they harvested the corn, drying as much as they could for the winter. In the fall, they traveled to the lakes and swamps to collect wild rice. When the weather grew cold, they moved into snug tents called tepees in the forest. During the long winter months, they hunted, ate the food they had stored, and sang songs and told stories.

Far away on the Atlantic Coast, waves of settlers were arriving from

Europe. These newcomers pushed out the Indians who lived there, forcing them west. Before any white people reached Minnesota, the Dakota felt their effects when a powerful Indian nation called the Ojibwe moved into Minnesota from the east. The Ojibwe, who are also known as the Anishinabe, began hunting and fishing on land used by the Dakota, and the two tribes fought. By 1880, the Ojibwe gained control of northern Minnesota. The Dakota moved south onto the Great Plains, where they became skilled horseback riders and buffalo hunters.

THE FUR TRADE

In 1660, a Frenchman named Pierre Radisson visited Minnesota. He wrote about the great opportunities to trade for furs with the Indians. Soon French and English traders were making the long journey to Minnesota. The English came from Hudson Bay, far to the north. The French came in canoes following the St. Lawrence River and the chain of Great Lakes.

The hardy French fur traders were called voyageurs. They got up at 4 or 5 A.M. and paddled until dark, not eating dinner until 9 or 10 P.M. They could travel almost anywhere in northern Minnesota by carrying their canoes from one lake to the next. These tiring walks were called portages. Even though the voyageurs' canoes were sometimes forty-five feet long, carrying them was not the hard part—their cargo weighed much more. The bundles of furs weighed ninety pounds each, and the men often carried two or three at a time. It was a rugged, exhausting life, but not without its pleasures for those who liked the wild out-of-doors.

BUILDING A STATE

In 1776, the American colonies declared their independence from England. When the United States bought a vast tract of land called the Louisiana Purchase in 1803, Minnesota became part of the young nation. In 1820, construction began on a fort where the Minnesota River joins the Mississippi. Fort Snelling housed the area's first school, hospital, library, and post office.

The fort was an outpost surrounded by wilderness—the nearest

Life at Fort Snelling was hard for the soldiers, who were stationed there for years without a break. Dr. Nathan Jarvis wrote home in 1834, "We have all been most of the month shut up in the fort and confin'd to our Rooms owing to the excessive cold."

town was three hundred miles away. In winter, when the rivers froze, no boats could reach the fort. Sometimes mail got through by dogsled, but in bad weather the people at the fort were completely cut off. In 1826, they received no mail for five months.

Two important settlements were started near Fort Snelling. Just to the north gushed the lovely Falls of St. Anthony, the only waterfall on the entire Mississippi River. American settlers used the rushing water to power sawmills and flour mills. The falls eventually became the center of a booming community called St. Anthony, which later became part of Minneapolis.

Just downriver from Fort Snelling was a community called Pig's Eye Landing, named after a saloonkeeper there. Pig's Eye Landing was the last place that a steamboat traveling upriver could safely stop; after that, the water was too shallow. Steamships eventually became the area's most important connection with the outside world. Whenever a steamboat docked, crowds gathered to greet the arrivals and hear the latest news. Pig's Eye Landing grew into the city of St. Paul.

Gradually, white Americans realized that Minnesota offered more than just furs. It also had plenty of forests that could be logged and fertile land that could be farmed. In 1837, the U.S. government pressured the Indians into giving up a big chunk of land between the Mississippi and St. Croix Rivers. In the next twenty years, the United States took control of most of the rest of the Indians' land in the region.

Minnesota grew rapidly during the 1850s. The territory's white population stood at 6,000 in 1850. By 1858, when Minnesota became a state, 150,000 people lived there. In 1854, the first com-

POPULATION GROWTH: 1850–2000

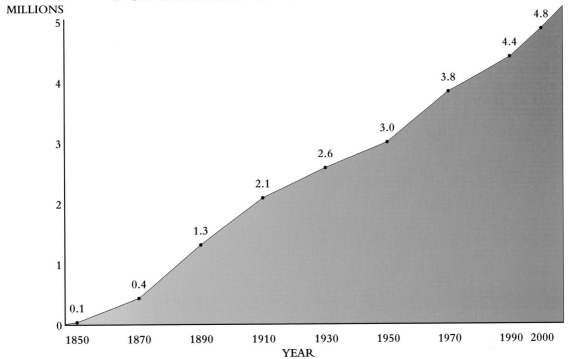

MILLIONS

5

4

3

2

1

0

0.1
0.4
1.3
2.1
2.6
3.0
3.8
4.4
4.8

1850 1870 1890 1910 1930 1950 1970 1990 2000

YEAR

mercial flour mill opened at the Falls of St. Anthony. By 1858, dozens of mills were harnessing the power of Minnesota's rivers, and by 1870 more than five hundred mills dotted the state. A decade later, Minneapolis was the major flour-milling city in the world.

TWO WARS

When the conflict between Northern and Southern states over slavery led to the Civil War in April 1861, Minnesota governor Alexander

In the nineteenth century, hundreds of mills that sawed lumber and ground flour were built along Minnesota's waterways. Minneapolis became the world's leading flour-milling city and the home of companies such as Pillsbury and General Mills.

Ramsey happened to be in Washington, D.C. He quickly offered one thousand men, making Minnesota the first state to volunteer troops for the Union cause. During the war, 24,000 Minnesotans went south to fight. One-tenth of them died.

While the country's attention was focused on Civil War battles in the South, fighting broke out back in Minnesota between whites and Indians. The Dakotas had been forced onto reservations along the Minnesota River that were not good for hunting. To survive, they depended on money and food that the U.S. government had promised them in exchange for their land. But little of the money was ever delivered, and by 1862, many Dakotas were starving.

The Dakotas believed that with so many soldiers off fighting the Civil War, they might be able to take back their land. A Dakota chief named Taoyateduta, or Little Crow, urged them to make peace. He realized they had no chance fighting against the entire United States. "You may kill one—two—ten; yes as many as the leaves in the forest. . . . Kill one—two—ten, and ten times ten will come to kill you," he told them. When his people decided to fight anyway, he said, "I am not a coward. I will die with you."

Bands of Dakotas went from farm to farm along the Minnesota River, burning buildings and killing entire families. Former Minnesota governor Henry Sibley led a group of soldiers who quickly crushed the rebellion. "We have inflicted so severe a blow upon the red devils that they will not dare to make another stand," he wrote his wife.

The captive Dakotas were brought to trial, and 303 were sentenced to death. President Abraham Lincoln ordered most of them freed, but 38 Dakotas were hung on December 26, 1862, in one of the largest mass executions in U.S. history.

After the Dakota War, life became much harder for all Indians in Minnesota. The Dakota's reservation along the Minnesota River was taken away, and most were sent to South Dakota, where many died of hunger and disease. Another tribe, the Winnebago, also lost their reservation even though they had no part in the war. Today, the Ojibwe are the only Indians in Minnesota with large reserva-

In 1862, the Dakota Indians attacked white settlers in the Minnesota River valley, the Indians' former home, after they had been cheated out of almost all the money promised them for selling their land.

tions. The Dakota, meanwhile, have just four small reservations in southern Minnesota.

HOMESTEADERS

The vast lands the government had obtained from the Indians soon opened to settlers. But farmers needed railroads to bring their goods to market. To encourage construction of the railroads, the government gave huge tracts of land to railroad companies—in fact, one-fifth of all the land in Minnesota.

Newspapers urged people to come to Minnesota and build new lives. In 1854, a *North-Western Democrat* article said, "Come on then; there is plenty of room—good prairie, good timber, good water and everything that an industrious and reasonable man could consider valuable, here awaits the careworn stranger from other parts of the world."

The Homestead Act in 1862 made it possible for pioneering settlers to get 160 acres of land free from the U.S. government. This enabled poor immigrants from Europe to come to America. Settlers claimed 1.25 million acres of land in Minnesota between 1863 and 1865. Many were immigrants from Germany and Ireland. Later, Swedes and Norwegians poured in. By 1880, one-third of Minnesotans were immigrants, and many more had foreign-born parents.

THE LOGGING BOOM

When white settlers began moving into Minnesota, two-thirds of the state was covered with trees. After the 1837 treaties with the Indians, loggers rushed in. Lumberjacks spent the cold winters cutting trees and dragging logs to the nearest river. When the ice melted, they stamped their company's mark on the logs and sent them floating downstream. Rivers such as the St. Croix sometimes got jammed with thousands of logs. When the logs arrived at mill towns, they were sawed into boards.

THE SHANTYMAN'S LIFE

During the Minnesota logging boom that peaked in the 1890s, thousands of men made their living cutting timber and hauling it out of the woods. Many loggers lived in crude huts called shanties. This song comes from the town of Bemidji.

Oh, a shan - ty - man's life is a wear - i - some life, al - though some think it void of care.

Swing - ing an ax from morn till night, in the midst of the for - ests drear.

Ly - ing in the shan - ty bleak and bare, while the cold storm - y win - try winds

blow. And as soon as day - light does ap -

pear, to the wild woods we must go.

Oh, the cook rises up in the middle of the night, saying "Hurrah, brave boys, it's day!"
Broken slumber ofttimes are passed as the cold winter night whiles away.
Had we rum, wine or beer our spirits to cheer, as the days so lonely do dwine,
Or a glass of any shone while in the woods alone for to cheer up our troubled minds.

But when spring does set in, double hardships begin, when the waters are piercing cold,
And our clothes are all wet, and fingers benumbed, and our pike-poles we scarcely can hold.
Betwixt rocks and shoals there's employment for all, as our well-banded raft we steer,
And the rapids that we run, oh, they seem to us but fun, for we're void of all slavish fear.

Oh, a brave shanty lad is the only lad I love, and I never will deny the same.
My heart doth scorn these conceited farmer boys, who think it a disgraceful name.
They may boast of their farms, but my shanty-boy's charms so far exceeds them all;
Until death doth part he shall enjoy my heart, let his riches be great or small.

During Minnesota's logging boom, lumberjacks shared large bunkhouses such as this one. Most loggers were unmarried, but some had to leave behind families on farms while they spent the winter in frigid logging camps.

The logging companies did not plan for the future; they just took all the logs they could get, leaving stumps and branches that sometimes burned in terrible fires. But while the logging boom lasted, it provided jobs for thousands, and made millionaires of the men who owned the companies. By the 1920s, when logging was petering out, a third of the state had been cleared of trees.

MINING

Stretching across northeastern Minnesota is a hundred-mile-long ridge that the Ojibwe called Mesabi, or Giant. A lumberman named Lewis Merritt was certain the Mesabi was filled with iron ore. He died in 1880 without finding any iron, but his seven sons kept searching. Although a mine opened in the nearby Vermilion Range in 1884, prospectors in the Mesabi found nothing but a lot of red dirt. Finally, in 1890, one of the Merritts' men had the dirt tested. It was two-thirds iron. Leonidas Merritt marveled, "If we had gotten mad and kicked the ground right where we stood, we would have thrown out 64-percent ore."

The Mahoning Mine, shown here in 1899, eventually became part of the giant Hull-Rust-Mahoning, the largest open-pit mine in the world. Many believe that the United States and its allies would not have been able to win either World War I or World War II without Minnesota's iron.

The Mesabi Range turned out to be the richest source of iron in the entire United States. In most of the country, deep mines had to be dug to reach the precious ore. In the Mesabi, the glaciers had already done most of the work. The ice floes had scraped off so much rock that in some places the iron lay right on the surface. By 1892, thousands of iron prospectors swarmed over the Mesabi. In 1893, Frank Hibbing led a group of men into the forest in search of iron. One cold January morning, Hibbing woke up and said, "My bones feel rusty. I believe there's iron under me." His bones were right, and a mining town called Hibbing soon sprang up on the spot.

Building miles of railroad tracks and fleets of ships to carry tons of ore to the steel mills in Pennsylvania required millions of dollars, and East Coast millionaires such as John D. Rockefeller and Andrew Carnegie quickly seized control of the iron industry in Minnesota. When the Merritts fell short of money in 1893, they lost their mining company to Rockefeller.

The big mining companies recruited laborers from Europe, and towns like Hibbing filled with people born in Finland, Italy, Croatia, and many other countries. The mining companies often owned the stores the miners shopped in and even the houses they lived in. When the miners tried to form unions, the companies sometimes hired thugs to beat them up. During a 1907 strike, a Finnish-American miner wrote to his brother, "There are 100 stooges with guns paid by the mining companies harassing the workers just like some animals."

Many miners were socialists, who thought the riches the mine owners were amassing should be shared by the workers. Polly Bullard, a young schoolteacher in the Iron Range, wrote in 1908 that her landlady was "a rabid Socialist and all the Socialists who come here to speak stay at her house. One came Saturday night and they had a grand to-do down in the kitchen till two in the morning." As the miners married and started families, they demanded that their towns become more than just a jumble of temporary shacks. Led by Victor Power, the "Fighting Mayor" of Hibbing, mining towns were able to provide services such as streetlights, schools, and hospitals by taxing the companies that were making millions from Minnesota's iron ore.

THE GRANGE MOVEMENT

Miners were not the only Minnesotans facing hardships. Minnesota farmers worked hard to raise animals and grow crops; all they wanted was a fair price for their efforts. But they needed railroads to transport their products to cities and had no choice but to pay whatever the railroads charged. They were also charged high prices to store their crops in huge towers called grain elevators. And if the big milling companies that turned their wheat into flour would only buy it at a low price, farmers had few places to turn. It seemed that no matter how hard the farmers worked, the railroads, elevators, and mills made most of the profits while the farmers struggled to break even.

The farmers responded by uniting to form big organizations of their own called cooperatives. Together, they could negotiate a better price or even buy their own elevators and mills. In the 1860s, a Minnesotan named Oliver Kelley had started a farmers' group called the Grange, which led a national movement for farmers'

In 1867, Minnesota farmer Oliver Kelley started the Grange Movement, which protected the rights of small farmers against big businesses. He was a lively, energetic man who said he was "as full of public spirit as a dog is full of fleas."

rights. Grange members fought for laws regulating how much the railroads could charge for shipping, shared new farming methods, and banded together to buy machinery at lower prices.

THE TWENTIETH CENTURY

Farming had its ups and downs. The low point hit during the Great Depression of the 1930s, when many farmers could not make any money at all. One farmer sent a six-hundred-pound hog to Chicago by train, but the railroad charged more to ship it than he made selling the pig. Prices for grain were so low that in 1932, some

A CLOUD OF BUGS

Some of the problems Minnesota farmers faced were more bizarre than low prices. For four years beginning in 1873, millions of grasshoppers invaded their fields and ate everything in sight, including clothes hanging out to dry. In her book, Laura Ingalls Wilder described how her father was just about to harvest his first wheat crop in Minnesota when the plague descended.

Plunk! Something hit Laura's head and fell to the ground. She looked down and saw the largest grasshopper she had ever seen. Then huge brown grasshoppers were hitting the ground all around her, hitting her head and her face and her arms. They came thudding down like hail.

The cloud was hailing grasshoppers. The cloud was grasshoppers. Their bodies hid the sun and made darkness. Their thin, large wings gleamed and glittered. The rasping whirring of their wings filled the whole air and they hit the ground and the house with the noise of a hailstorm.

Laura tried to beat them off. Their claws clung to her skin and her dress. They looked at her with bulging eyes, turning their heads this way and that. Mary ran screaming into the house. Grasshoppers covered the ground, there was not one bare bit to step on. Laura had to step on grasshoppers and they smashed squirming and slimy under her feet.

farmers went on strike. They blocked the roads, refusing to allow food into the cities.

Many farmers lost more than money—they lost their farms. Oftentimes, they had borrowed money to buy land. When the price of corn fell from eighty to ten cents a bushel, there was no way they

During the Great Depression, farmers went on strike. In 1933, they marched on the state capitol in St. Paul and won passage of a law that stopped banks from taking farms away from people who owed them money.

could earn enough to repay the loans. The banks took back the farms and auctioned them off. Some farmers tried to prevent these sales by threatening judges and sheriffs. Others crowded the auctions and bought the farm, tools, and animals for mere pennies; anyone who tried to bid more was warned to keep silent. Having bought a farm at one of these "penny auctions," the farmers would simply give it back to the original owner.

Many other people also suffered during the Great Depression. Two-thirds of Minnesota's iron miners lost their jobs, and one in three factory workers in the Twin Cities was laid off.

In 1918, some workers and small farmers had started their own political party, called the Farmer-Labor Party, because they believed that neither the Democrats nor the Republicans did enough to help them. The Farmer-Labor Party reached full flower in the 1930s, when Minnesota's governor, both its U.S. senators, and the majority of the state legislature were all party members.

The Depression ended with World War II, when Minnesota's miners supplied iron for America's war effort, and farmers provided food for soldiers. In 1944, the Democratic Party merged with the Farmer-Labor Party. Though not as radical as the old Farmer-Labor Party, the Democratic-Farmer-Labor Party (DFL) produced such popular liberal politicians as Hubert H. Humphrey, who was a leader in the national movement for civil rights. In 1964, Humphrey was elected vice president of the United States. Another DFL senator, Walter Mondale, was elected vice president in 1976.

The DFL's power has waned since the 1970s, and Republicans have gained ground in the state. In 1998, Minnesota voters shocked the nation by electing former professional wrestler Jesse "the Body" Ventura of the Reform Party as their governor, proving that the tradition of looking beyond the two major parties is alive and well in Minnesota.

3 WORKING TOGETHER

The capitol in St. Paul

Minnesotans believe in traditional values such as civic responsibility and lending a hand to a neighbor. Though they may seem old-fashioned, they are not afraid to try new ideas. Minnesota has led the way on many reforms in education, environmental protection, and law enforcement.

INSIDE GOVERNMENT

Minnesota's government has three branches: executive, legislative, and judicial.

Executive. The head of the executive branch is the governor, who serves a four-year term. The governor appoints people to important positions on commissions and in state departments. He or she signs laws passed by the legislature or blocks them with a veto. The legislature can override a veto if two-thirds of its members agree.

Legislative. The legislature consists of a senate with 67 members who serve four-year terms, and a house of representatives with 134 members who serve two-year terms. The legislature makes laws, sets taxes, and controls the state budget.

Judicial. The state's highest court is the supreme court, composed of seven judges elected to six-year terms. Beneath it are the

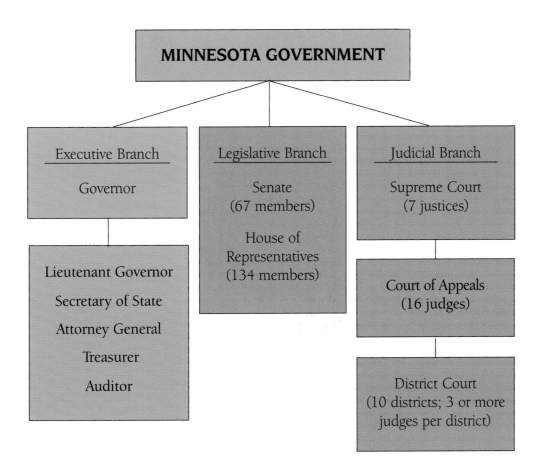

MINNESOTA GOVERNMENT

Executive Branch

Governor

Lieutenant Governor

Secretary of State

Attorney General

Treasurer

Auditor

Legislative Branch

Senate
(67 members)

House of
Representatives
(134 members)

Judicial Branch

Supreme Court
(7 justices)

Court of Appeals
(16 judges)

District Court
(10 districts; 3 or more
judges per district)

court of appeals, district courts, county courts, municipal courts, and justices of the peace. Decisions of lower courts can be appealed to higher courts for review, all the way up to the supreme court.

Minnesota's best-known judge is Alan Page, one of the greatest football players in history. As a member of the powerful Minnesota Vikings team that played in four Super Bowls, Page became the first defensive player ever named the league's Most Valuable Player. Page attended law school between football seasons, and when he retired from the sport he became a lawyer and then a judge. He is now a Minnesota Supreme Court justice. Page has spoken to thousands

As a member of the "Purple People Eaters," the Minnesota Vikings' feared defensive line of the 1970s, Alan Page became the first defensive player ever to win the National Football League's Most Valuable Player award. Page attended law school between football seasons and went on to become a Minnesota Supreme Court justice.

of schoolchildren, reminding them that their education is a lot more important than sports.

SUPPORTING SCHOOLS

Minnesotans are proud of their commitment to keeping Minnesota a nice place to live for everyone. "We are not like a lot of other states. We want to be thought of as a very progressive state, but we don't want to be thought of as a big state. We're willing to pay more taxes for certain things, and we're very prideful of those things," says prominent businessman Glen Taylor.

Minnesotans pay some of the highest taxes of any state. One

thing Minnesotans get for their high taxes is an excellent school system. Minnesota ranks near the top in the percentage of students who graduate from high school, and its high-school graduates rank among the top five states in college admission test scores. Almost half the state budget goes to education.

Another reason for the schools' success is a willingness to exper-

Two children wait for the school bus in a farming community in southwestern Minnesota.

iment. The Twin Cities offer many different types of schools, and families can choose which approach is best for their kids. As the Minneapolis schools superintendent proudly explained, "We have more choices. In this district you can go to an open school, a Montessori school, a continuous-progress school, a regular school, a math-science-technology school, a language-immersion school, a liberal-arts magnet, an aerospace magnet, a fine-arts magnet."

HELPING EACH OTHER

Minnesotans' commitment to taking care of each other and their community has not made them immune to problems. But they try to respond in creative ways that consider the needs of all. For instance, in 1996, new federal laws forced people off welfare in hopes they would start working to support themselves. Although Minnesota pushed people to find work, it also supplied money to solve the problems that prevented them from working. "If it's child care, let's connect you with the basic sliding-fee child care so you can avoid going on welfare. If it's because your car broke down, then let's fix the car," said Deborah Huskings of the Minnesota Department of Human Services.

FIGHTING CRIME

In the mid-1990s, Minnesotans—used to seeing themselves as peaceful and law-abiding—were stunned when the murder rate in Minneapolis soared. Criminal gangs were moving into the city, and

EARNING A LIVING

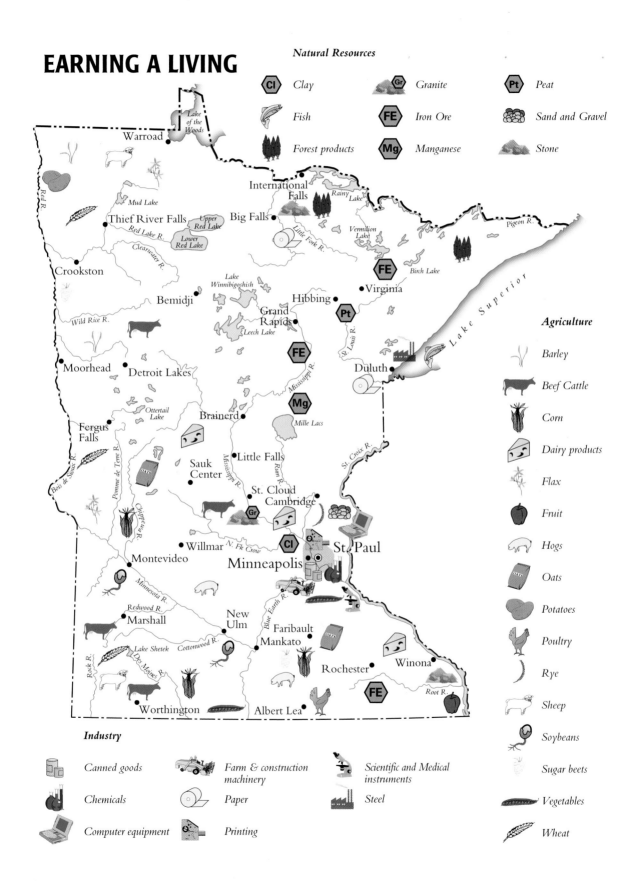

Natural Resources

- **Cl** Clay
- Fish
- Forest products
- **Gr** Granite
- **FE** Iron Ore
- **Mg** Manganese
- **Pt** Peat
- Sand and Gravel
- Stone

Agriculture

- Barley
- Beef Cattle
- Corn
- Dairy products
- Flax
- Fruit
- Hogs
- Oats
- Potatoes
- Poultry
- Rye
- Sheep
- Soybeans
- Sugar beets
- Vegetables
- Wheat

Industry

- Canned goods
- Chemicals
- Computer equipment
- Farm & construction machinery
- Paper
- Printing
- Scientific and Medical instruments
- Steel

Warroad
Lake of the Woods
International Falls
Rainy Lake
Mud Lake
Thief River Falls
Big Falls
Upper Red Lake
Lower Red Lake
Red Lake R.
Clearwater R.
Little Fork R.
Vermilion Lake
Pigeon R.
Crookston
Birch Lake
Virginia
Bemidji
Lake Winnibigoshish
Hibbing
Grand Rapids
St. Louis R.
Wild Rice R.
Leech Lake
FE
Pt
Lake Superior
Moorhead
Detroit Lakes
FE
Duluth
Mississippi R.
Ottertail Lake
Brainerd
Mg
Mille Lacs
Fergus Falls
Bois de Sioux R.
Pomme de Terre R.
Sauk Center
Little Falls
Mississippi R.
Rum R.
St. Croix R.
Chippewa R.
St. Cloud
Cambridge
Gr
Willmar
N. Fk. Crow R.
Cl
St. Paul
Montevideo
Minneapolis
Minnesota R.
Redwood R.
Marshall
New Ulm
Blue Earth R.
Faribault
Mankato
Rochester
Winona
Lake Shetek
Cottonwood R.
Rock R.
Des Moines R.
FE
Root R.
Worthington
Albert Lea

a third of the inmates in Minneapolis's Hennepin County jail had lived in Minnesota for less than five years. Minneapolis responded to this influx of criminals by targeting gangs and people who committed crimes while out on parole for other convictions. Previously, those who violated parole faced few consequences. Now, repeat offenders quickly found themselves back in jail. Over the next few years, the murder rate dropped sharply.

But true to its liberal traditions, Minneapolis did not stop at simply "getting tough" on crime. The city also worked hard to prevent kids from turning to crime in the first place. School programs, recreation programs, and neighborhood block clubs were all enlisted to provide healthy options for kids. While other states responded to crime by simply building more prisons, Minnesota's corrections commissioner, Fred LaFleur, insisted that Minnesota "can't build our way out of the situation—that's folly." He argues it is cheaper and more effective to help troubled families by offering parenting classes and skills training. "There's going to be crime in our community," said Minneapolis police chief Robert Olson. "But a lot of it doesn't have to happen if the community, the government and the neighborhoods join hands and fight this."

BREAD AND BUTTER

Many Minnesotans still work in the state's traditional industries of farming, mining, and tourism. But newer industries such as banking and computer and electronics manufacturing thrive in Minnesota as well, particularly in the Twin Cities area, where more than half the state's population lives.

School superintendent Peter Hutchinson says that in Minneapolis, "Your child can go to school with children from all over the world, who speak many different languages, who bring their cultures to school with them every day."

South and central Minnesota still contain some of the nation's best farmland. Minnesota produces so many grain and dairy products that it is often called the Bread and Butter State. While the Falls of St. Anthony are no longer surrounded by flour mills, the world's four largest milling companies still maintain their headquarters in Minneapolis. The shelves of almost every supermarket in the country hold flour from Minnesota companies such as Pillsbury and General Mills, as well as Land O' Lakes butter. Minnesota produces more dairy

Minnesota's bountiful harvests of grain and dairy products have earned it the nickname the Bread and Butter State.

products than any state except Wisconsin. It ranks among the top five states in the production of oats, sugar beets, corn, barley, soybeans, and turkeys. Wheat, potatoes, and apples are also important crops.

Factories throughout Minnesota process these goods into flour, butter, cheese, oil, and sugar, as well as breakfast cereal and cake

MIGHTY MOMS IN THE MALL

The Mall of America in suburban Minneapolis is the biggest mall in the United States, and in 1996 it had a big problem. It had become too popular for its own good. Thousands of teenagers came each weekend, and they were getting out of hand. Though most behaved well, some would gather in large groups and curse, fight, or drop food onto people's heads from the balconies above.

To combat this problem, the mall tried something new: it hired twenty local moms. Consultant Richard Mammen explained the idea, "We know some kids don't respond well to authority figures, especially ones in uniform. But usually they will listen to a mom."

"It's hard to be a jerk to a mom," admitted sixteen-year-old Jenny Mohn. "I got stopped last night outside of Bloomingdale's by a security guard, and I got mad and gave him some attitude. But with the Moms it's like, 'O.K., I'll do what you want.'"

With the help of the Mighty Moms and a teen curfew on weekends, crime plummeted. Mall spokeswoman Teresa McFarland marveled, "Last year at this time there would be ten kids arrested every weekend for fighting, and now we have none."

The program—the first of its kind in the nation—is now being considered by other malls. "Mighty Mom" Va-Lesha Beeks summed it up, "Sometimes you need the authority of a security officer to make things right, and sometimes you just need a mom."

mixes. Factories also turn out nonfood products such as paper, books, and computers. Polaris, the world's biggest snowmobile manufacturer, employs 1,800 people in Roseau. Almost as many work for rival Arctic Cat in Thief River Falls.

Even though the Iron Range still produces two-thirds of the

FARM STATE FUN

If you're lucky enough to be in the Twin Cities in late August, you can join the 1.5 million people who visit the Minnesota State Fair each year. The fair has all the traditional attractions including cotton candy, carnival rides, and prize-winning pickles and pies, plus unique Minnesota treats such as "walleye on a stick"—an original way to enjoy one of Minnesota's most popular fish, the walleye. You can also try a popular snack in dairy country: deep-fried cheese curds. Leo Berg, president of the Minnesota Festivals and Events Association, says that at a fair, "people like to eat something they are not going to eat every day of the year."

There are 15,000 animals at the fair, from llamas to horses, pigs, sheep, and chickens of every imaginable color—and of course, cows. In the Moo Booth, a dairy farmer tells visitors that "a 1,400-pound cow will eat enough to produce 115 pounds of manure every day." Other cow-related attractions include a life-size human head carved from an eighty-five-pound hunk of butter, and a tanker truck that sells all the fresh milk you can drink for fifty cents.

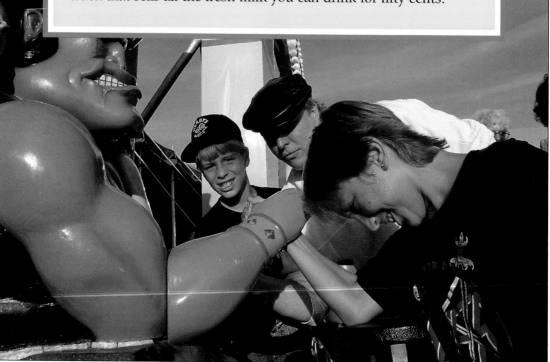

Minnesota produces more turkeys than any other state.

nation's iron ore, thousands of miners lost their jobs in the 1980s, and mining alone can no longer support northern Minnesota's economy. Tourism is a key source of jobs in the north, where Voyageurs National Park and the Boundary Waters Canoe Area Wilderness preserve hundreds of unspoiled lakes. People come from all over the country to canoe in the Boundary Waters, where motorboats are not allowed on most lakes.

GROSS STATE PRODUCT: $160 BILLION

(2000 estimated)

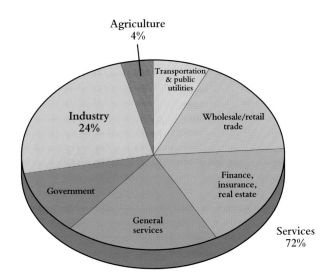

Agriculture
4%

Transportation
& public
utilities

Industry
24%

Wholesale/retail
trade

Government

Finance,
insurance,
real estate

General
services

Services
72%

Some people who live nearby resent the ban on motorboats. They believe these restrictions limit the amount of money they can earn from tourism. Fortunately, many vacationers come precisely because of the rules against motorboats, and tourism is thriving. But the battle still rages over using motorboats on the park's border lakes. For now, the Boundary Waters remains one of the few places in America where you can canoe all day and hear only the splash of your paddle, the rustle of the wind in the trees, and perhaps the laughing call of a loon.

The Boundary Waters Canoe Area Wilderness is one of the best places in the world to enjoy nature. Motorboats are not allowed in most of the wild, lake-filled region.

4 LIFE IN THE NORTHLAND

If you didn't know anything about Minnesotans, you might think that when they put "10,000 Lakes" on their license plates, they were bragging. But the truth is, they were being modest. Minnesota actually has nearly 12,000 lakes of at least ten acres, and if smaller lakes are included, the total is more than 15,000. It is typical of Minnesotans, according to writer Steve Rushin, to have "rounded the number down." Rushin also found it telling that when a new skyscraper, the Norwest Center, was built in downtown Minneapolis, it was intentionally built a few feet shorter than the nearby IDS Center to keep it from becoming the state's tallest building.

MINNESOTA NICE

According to Minnesota writer Garrison Keillor, this modesty is characteristic of "a state of Germans and Scandinavians who believe in hard work, perseverance, and don't think you're somebody special, because you're not." Minnesotans have a reputation for being patient, humble, and extremely polite. The phrase "Minnesota nice" is used to describe their famous courtesy.

A New York reporter once described Minnesotans as "so polite it can sometimes be maddening." In his book *How to Talk Minnesotan*, humorist Howard Mohr jokes that a real Minnesotan will never accept food until the third offer. He includes as practice dialogue:

The ancestors of many Minnesotans came from Norway and Sweden, which have climates similar to Minnesota's. Hardy Minnesotans enjoy the cold weather by going cross-country skiing, snowshoeing, or even winter camping.

"Want a cup of coffee before you go?"

"No, I wouldn't want to put you out. I'll get by."

"You sure? Just made a fresh pot."

"You didn't have to go and do that."

"How about it, one cup?"

"Well, if it's going to hurt your feelings, but don't fill it full."

This mild-mannered, low-key quality can be confusing to outsiders. One transplanted New Yorker, Barbara Graham, complained that when talking to a native Minnesotan, "'Yah, then, I'm not feelin' too good' might well mean, 'Help! I'm having a heart attack!'" Others complain that being "nice" all the time means never saying what you are really feeling. Many people give as an example "the old Swedish farmer who loved his wife so much he nearly told her."

Would every Minnesotan you meet sound like the people in these jokes? As with any stereotype, the answer is no, of course not. If they reveal anything, it is probably that Minnesotans love poking fun at themselves.

FROM FARAWAY LANDS

The stereotype of Minnesota as a land of Scandinavians and Germans is partly true: the state's three largest ethnic groups are Germans, Swedes, and Norwegians. But many other groups, such as the descendants of Finnish, Italian, and Eastern European immigrants who came to work in the Iron Range, also populate the state. Many Irish people settled in the Red River valley, and some farm towns are filled with people of Czech and Polish heritage. But while European Americans are still the vast majority, things are changing, as immigrants flock in from Asia and Africa.

In the 1960s, during the Vietnam War, the U.S. government recruited Hmong people living along the border between Laos and Vietnam to help them. When the U.S. pulled out of Vietnam, the Hmong were left at the mercy of their enemies, and thousands were killed. Church groups in Minnesota invited Hmong refugees to the Twin Cities, and from the 1970s to the 1990s, about 40,000 came. It was a very difficult adjustment for these newcomers. Su Thao

SWEDISH MEATBALLS

This dish of meatballs in a creamy sauce was brought to Minnesota by Scandinavian immigrants. Today, it is popular throughout the state. Have an adult help you with this recipe.

½ cup milk
1 egg, slightly beaten
2 slices bread, crusts removed
1 pound lean ground beef
¼ pound ground pork
2 tablespoons finely minced onions
1 teaspoon salt
½ teaspoon sugar
½ teaspoon black pepper
4 tablespoons butter
1 can condensed cream of chicken soup
½ can condensed tomato soup
½ soup can warm water

1. Combine milk and egg. Add bread, torn into chunks. Set aside to soak.

2. Mince the onions. Combine with beef, pork, salt, sugar, and pepper in large bowl. Mix lightly with hands. Add egg mixture and mix thoroughly.

3. Shape into small meatballs about the size of walnuts.

4. Heat butter in frying pan over medium heat. Brown meatballs, turning often to keep them round. Do not crowd pan.

5. Remove meatballs from pan. Add chicken soup, tomato soup, and water to pan and stir thoroughly.

6. Place meatballs in a casserole dish. Pour sauce over top and bake 20 minutes at 350 degrees.

Hmong refugees learn American agricultural methods at the University of Minnesota. More Hmong now live in Minnesota than in their home country of Laos.

remembers stepping off a plane as a young boy in subzero weather wearing only sandals on his feet. In Laos, he had hunted in the mountains and rode a water buffalo to school. In Minnesota, he joined a Boy Scout troop and became the first Hmong Eagle Scout. Congressman Bruce Vento said, "I'm very proud of the fact that in St. Paul schools about 30 percent . . . are Southeast Asian. . . . They are going to be leaders in my state and they're going to be leaders in this country."

In the 1990s, Minnesotans reached out to other immigrant groups, including Somalis, Ethiopians, Eritreans, and Koreans. Adele Starr, a nurse practitioner in Minneapolis, says that her clinic needs five full-time translators. "We have two Hmong/Laotian interpreters, one Somali interpreter, one Vietnamese interpreter, one Cambodian interpreter, and several people on our staff speak Spanish. It's like working in the United Nations. It's so interesting."

The influx of people from around the world has made Minneapolis much more cosmopolitan. In 1970, the city was 93 percent white. By 1990, the minority population had risen to 22 percent, and it continued to increase in the 1990s. By 1998, 68 percent of Minneapolis's public school children were nonwhite, and they spoke seventy-one different languages. "This is not your grandfather's Minneapolis," says Emmett Carson, an African American who is president of the Minneapolis Foundation. "We're not a small town anymore. We're becoming a big city."

The newcomers have also spiced up the local cuisine. Twin Cities residents now have their pick of Mexican, Ethiopian, and Vietnamese restaurants. "Bland is boring. This is really cool," said Dale Hall of the squid, boiled quail eggs, and jelly grass he had just purchased from a Vietnamese food market. In the rest of the state, however, eating out still means having a piece of pie in a small-town diner.

Over the years, Minnesota's American Indians have struggled with poverty and adjusting to new traditions. Some still collect wild rice on their reservation land, but more live off-reservation. Operating gambling casinos provides many Native Americans with an important source of income. "Now that we have casinos, more people are moving back to the reservation. . . . Which is good, because now we have a little bit more of an Indian community than we had before," says Brenda Moose Boyd, whose Ojibwe name is Niizhoogaabawiikwe.

CELEBRATING TOGETHER

Minnesotans celebrate their many different traditions with hundreds of festivals. In addition to a Festival of Nations in St. Paul celebrating ninety-five different ethnic groups, there are festivals for individual groups including Czech Kolacky Days in Montgomery; a

A young dancer at an American Indian powwow in Grand Portage

Dancers celebrate their Swedish heritage at Svenskarnas Dag, or Swedes Day, in Minneapolis. So many Scandinavians immigrated to Minnesota that two counties north of St. Paul became known as Swedeland, USA.

German Oktoberfest in New Ulm; an Ojibwe powwow at the Mille Lacs Reservation; and Syttende Mai, a Norwegian independence day celebration in Wanamingo featuring a lutefisk dinner. (Lutefisk, a Norwegian dish made of fish soaked in lye, has achieved legendary status in Minnesota.) Other Minnesota festivals highlight traditional activities such as quilting, polka dancing, and wood carving. But many are simply for fun. In all, Minnesotans turn out for 1,600 festivals each year. A real fan could attend Willie Walleye Day, Sheep Days, Tater Days, Spudfest, Turtle Fest, Bean Hole Days, Sawdust Dayz, Stinker Days, Blueberry Art Festival, Pie Day, Eggstravaganza, Old Time Fiddle Championship, Ox Cart Days, and the Western Minnesota Steam Threshers Reunion.

For many, a festival is simply a way to see old friends and celebrate small-town life. The North Morristown Picnic has been a Fourth of July tradition for more than one hundred years. "There aren't too many places like this any more," said a woman from Kilkenny who came to dance to the polka music of the Six Fat Dutchmen. "I think that a lot of people like to go back to the more traditional celebrations their parents and grandparents had." Don Preuss of Waseca has been coming to the picnic for sixty years. "It's a real family-oriented deal," he said. "I think the church and school really help hold it together."

OUTDOOR FUN

Even in the heart of winter, Minnesotans aren't afraid to go outside and play. Journalist Dan Kaercher once wrote, "I'm still amazed at a simple fact of life in our region: The farther north you go, the more fun people have in winter." Pointing to a frozen lake, Minnesotan Jane Gunsbury explains, "We have all this extra room in the winter. Might as well have fun with it!"

One thing many Minnesotans like to do is ride snowmobiles, which were invented in northern Minnesota. The state contains more than 18,000 miles of snowmobile trails. Betsy Hollister runs

"PLEASE DO NOT DRILL HOLES IN THE ROADS"

Most people would be squeamish about driving their car out onto a frozen lake—and rightly so. But when the ice is three feet thick, as it can be in Minnesota, it's too inviting for some to pass up. Because under all that ice fish are swimming around. All you have to do is chop a hole, and you can go ice-fishing.

Since it's too cold to sit outside all day, most ice-fishermen drag buildings out on the ice and fish through holes in the floor. These shacks range from homemade plywood-and-tarpaper shanties to heated, carpeted houses. Ice-fisherman Jim Mackenthun can fish from his shanty while lying in bed and listening to the radio. While small lakes may sprout just a few old shacks, on Mille Lacs Lake, five thousand ice-fishing houses form a good-sized town. Neat roads are shoveled through the snow, and the buildings have driveways and street addresses. A road map warns ice-fishermen, "Please do not drill holes in the roads."

Several lakes offer ice-fishing contests, where for a dollar anyone willing to sit outdoors can try their luck. At Gull Lake, nearly six thousand people pay $30 to trudge out on the ice in below-zero weather for the annual $100,000 Ice Fishing Extravaganza. They huddle over their fishing holes, trying to keep warm with propane heaters or by dancing to music broadcast over loudspeakers. As Bob Michael said of his fellow ice-fishermen, "This is behavior that's unique."

An artist fashions an ice sculpture with a chainsaw at the St. Paul Winter Carnival.

(Top right) The tradition of building castles made of ice for the St. Paul Winter Carnival goes back more than one hundred years. This modern ice castle, glowing with colored lights, towered 150 feet in the air.

A family relaxes by the lake in Voyageurs National Park.

a coffeehouse in Nisswa along a one-hundred-mile route from Brainerd to Bemidji where snowmobilers stop and warm up by a fire. "Hot soup, hot coffee, and they're off. They can't wait to get back out there," she says.

Less noisy winter sports include showshoeing and cross-country skiing. For something different, you can put on some skis, strap yourself to a sled dog, and go skijoring. "It's like waterskiing, but the boat is a dog, and the snow is the water," explains Shari Baker, who works at the Gunflint Lodge, which rents skijoring equipment.

Minnesota is the biggest hockey state in the country, which is not really surprising—in the winter, you can hose down a football field or shovel off a frozen lake, and you've got a hockey rink. Minnesota has more than two thousand amateur hockey clubs and has turned out more professional and Olympic hockey players than any other state. Most U.S. colleges need to import players from Canada for their teams, but the University of Minnesota once won a national championship with a team composed entirely of players born in Minnesota.

In January, the St. Paul Winter Carnival offers ski and snowmobile races. But throughout the carnival's more than one-hundred-year history, the greatest attraction has always been the towering castles made entirely of ice. When lit up at night, these dazzling crystal palaces glow like a sight from a fairy tale. Years ago, visitors could go inside these castles. Some contained ballrooms, skating rinks, and several floors. One even had an elevator. In 1992, the celebration featured an ice castle 150 feet tall—the largest ever made.

In summer, Minnesotans make full use of their lakes. Three-quarters of a million boats are registered in Minnesota—one for every six people—and one of every four Minnesotans has a fishing license. According to one poll, six of ten adult Minnesotans made an overnight trip to a lake within the past year. For many residents, "a dock, a lake, a cabin, and a fishing boat is kind of like standard equipment," says Minnesota native Chris Stellar.

Those who can't afford to buy their own cabin on a lake can stay at one of the state's more than one thousand resorts. For many families, going to a resort is simpler than taking care of a place year-round. Many families go back to the same site year after year, until it feels like home. "Cabin 12 just feels like part of our family," says Liz VanderAarde of Burnsville.

But for many, including magazine editor Bonnie Blodgett, it "seems like almost everybody we know who grew up here in Minnesota still has a lake place in the family. Or a friend who does. And there's always room on the floor for another sleeping bag."

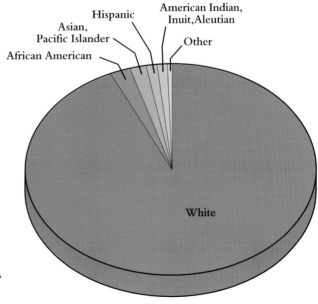

ETHNIC MINNESOTA

5 MINNESOTA VISIONS

Minnesotans have achieved success in every field. The following are just a few of the Minnesotans who have made their mark on the world stage.

THE MAYO DOCTORS

Minnesota's Mayo brothers are probably the most famous doctors in U.S. history. Their father, William Worrall Mayo, was born in England and came to America in 1845 to study medicine. He started working as a doctor in Minnesota in 1855 and gained a reputation as a skilled surgeon. Mayo was one of the first doctors to use a microscope to hunt for disease. In 1863, he moved to Rochester. His sons, William and Charles, born in 1861 and 1865, began visiting patients with him at age twelve. They eventually became surgeons, too.

In 1889, the Mayos began running a hospital in Rochester, where the two brothers performed all the surgery until about 1905. The Mayo brothers were superb surgeons, and patients came hundreds of miles to be cured. Doctors came too, to watch the operations. One amazed doctor watched them do a hundred operations in six days; another saw Will do ten operations in one morning. Together, the Mayo brothers did almost four thousand operations in one year.

Gradually, more doctors were added, and the hospital grew and

The famous Mayo brothers, Charles and William, and their father, William Worrall Mayo, made the Mayo Clinic in Rochester, Minnesota, one of the world's leading medical institutions.

grew. Today, more than 400,000 patients come each year from all over the world to be treated by two thousand doctors at the Mayo Clinic, one of the world's greatest medical facilities.

MINNESOTA WRITERS

The Minnesota childhoods of two of America's most esteemed writers, Sinclair Lewis and F. Scott Fitzgerald, had lasting effects on their work. Although both wrote their most important novels in the 1920s, their points of view were completely different.

Sinclair Lewis grew up in Sauk Centre, a small town in western Minnesota, where he was shy and unpopular. Later, Lewis developed a gift for mimicking people and could parody them like a stand-up comic. The son of a strict, hardworking doctor, Lewis fled the confinement of his hometown. Although he spent much of his life traveling, visiting forty states and seventeen countries, most of his books describe his midwestern roots.

Sinclair Lewis was the first American to win the Nobel Prize for literature. Critic H. L. Mencken wrote in praise of Lewis's novel Babbitt, "I know of no American novel that more accurately presents the real America."

Lewis's 1920 novel, *Main Street*, concerns an idealistic young woman who dreams of bringing beauty and culture to a town named Gopher Prairie, modeled after Sauk Centre. But the town's rigid, small-minded citizens wear her down and break her spirit. In *Babbitt*, Lewis attacked phony, self-satisfied behavior in a bigger city. The main character, George Babbitt, has all the things he is supposed to want—a house, a car, a family, success in business, and a respected place in the community—but his life is hollow and meaningless. The word *Babbitt* has entered the dictionary as a symbol of mindless conformity. In novel after novel, Lewis exposed aspects of American life that others avoided. He punctured the myth of wholesome, small-town life and changed the way America saw itself. In 1930, he became the first American writer to receive the Nobel Prize, the world's highest literary honor.

Sauk Centre's residents have forgiven Lewis for his critical descriptions of life on Main Street. They now celebrate Sinclair Lewis Days each summer, and the high school teams are named the Mainstreeters.

If asked to name a single "great American novel," many would pick F. Scott Fitzgerald's *The Great Gatsby*. This book perfectly expresses the dreams and illusions of a country in which the wealthy live in a glamorous world above the rest. Fitzgerald was born into a well-off St. Paul family. He attended private schools, where he acted in plays and wrote for school publications. His first novel, *This Side of Paradise*, about an idealistic college student, quickly made Fitzgerald famous, and he spent the 1920s living the whirlwind life he described in his stories. But his high living took its toll, and by the 1930s he was in debt and struggling with

Author F. Scott Fitzgerald wrote during the freewheeling Jazz Age of the 1920s. World War I had just ended, and as Fitzgerald put it, "America was going on the greatest, gaudiest spree in history and there was going to be plenty to tell about it."

alcoholism. He died of a heart attack in 1940 at age forty-four. At the time, his novels were not selling well, and he considered himself "a forgotten man." But his reputation has continued to grow. Today, half a million copies of Fitzgerald's books are sold each year, and he ranks among the greatest writers of the century.

Artist and writer Wanda Gag is best known for her brilliant children's book *Millions of Cats*, which was published in 1928. In her drawing and her life, Gag expressed a passionate spirit and defiant independence.

Gag grew up in New Ulm, Minnesota. Her father was a painter, and the family spent their evenings drawing together around the kitchen table. When Gag was fifteen, her father died, and her family was suddenly very poor. As the oldest of seven children, Wanda had to help support the family, earning money making art for cards, fabrics, toys, and newspapers.

Gag was so passionate about art, sometimes she would stay up all night, unable to ignore "that fiery thing inside which was always trying to get out and which made me draw so furiously." Her intensity shows in her pictures: no matter how simple the subject, every line seems to be alive and pulsing with energy.

Though critics loved her artwork, her fame comes mostly from the children's books she wrote and illustrated, including *Snippy and Snappy* and *Nothing-at-All*. Gag also translated and illustrated three volumes of Grimms' fairy tales. In 1940, she published *Growing Pains*, a description of her childhood that captures her sense of wonder and excitement as a young artist.

FROM FOLK TO FUNK

When legendary folk-rock artist Bob Dylan started out, most musicians did not write their own songs. Dylan changed that forever. By voicing political protest and every possible emotion in his deeply personal, poetic lyrics, he raised rock 'n' roll from bouncy dance music to a potent art form. He expressed a restlessness, frustration, and a sense of boundless possibility that changed the way people saw rock music—and their lives.

Bob Dylan was born Robert Zimmerman in 1941 and grew up on

the Iron Range, in Hibbing. He once shocked his classmates at a high-school talent show by wailing out tunes he had picked up from late-night Chicago rhythm and blues stations. After graduating in 1959, he couldn't wait to leave town. He enrolled in the University of Minnesota but spent most of his time playing folk music in coffee-houses. "I had already decided that society, as it was, was pretty phony and I didn't want to be part of that," he said. He remembered, "There was a lot of unrest in the country. You could feel it, a lot of frustration, sort of like a calm before a hurricane, things were shaking up."

Dylan moved to New York and soon became a fixture in small clubs, where he sang classic folk songs his own way, with a harsh, insistent voice. He said later, "I played all the folk songs with a rock 'n' roll attitude."

When he started writing his own songs, people were stunned. "The Times They Are A-Changin'," "Blowin' in the Wind," and "Masters of War" lit a fire under the whole country. The 1960s were a time of great upheaval in America, as young people protested the Vietnam War and pushed for civil rights. Folk music became a rallying cry for change, and Dylan found himself at the center of a movement.

But at the 1965 Newport Folk Festival, he drew boos from folk purists by appearing in a black leather jacket with an electric guitar and a band that blasted out loud rock versions of his songs. He began traveling with a wild, freeform band that left even rock audiences confused. His style would catch on a few years later—but by then, Dylan had moved on to something else. By the late 1970s, when seemingly nothing was too shocking for rock audi-

Bob Dylan remembers that when he left Minnesota to hitchhike to New York City, he "stood on the highway during a blizzard snowstorm . . . didn't have nothing but my guitar and suitcase."

ences, Dylan managed to stun his fans once again with his deeply religious albums. Today, Dylan continues to command attention. In 1998, he won three Grammies for the brooding, gloomy *Time Out of Mind*.

After spawning the most important American singer of the 1960s in Bob Dylan, Minnesota produced one of the most influential stars of the 1980s, the Artist Formerly Known as Prince. Born Prince Rogers Nelson in 1958, this musical genius went by the name Prince until 1993, when he changed his name to a symbol.

Prince grew up in predominantly black North Minneapolis. While still a teenager, he astonished critics by producing an album on which he sang, wrote all the music, and played all of the instruments. Within a year he had produced a second album and a number-one soul hit "I Wanna Be Your Lover." In 1982, Prince hit the big time with *1999*, which sold three million copies. Two years later he starred in the hit movie *Purple Rain*. Its sound track sold more than 11 million copies, making Prince one of the biggest stars of the decade.

Prince's music took the irresistible grooves of the funk dance

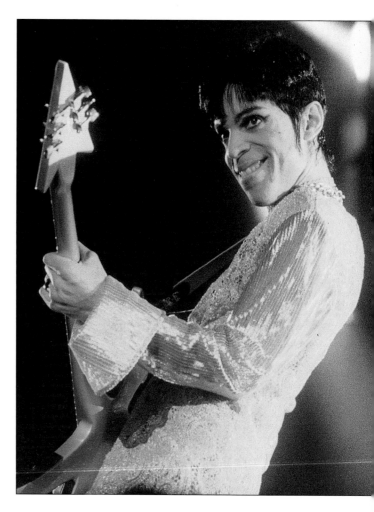

The Artist Formerly Known as Prince constantly experiments with new musical styles, but he continues to write hit songs, sometimes giving them to other singers to help launch their careers.

music popular in the 1970s and made them faster, tenser, and leaner, replacing horns with tight, punchy bursts from his synthesizer. You can turn on the radio today and still hear music that sounds like a poor imitation of the "Minneapolis Sound" Prince developed twenty years ago. Prince still lives in Minnesota, where he built his own recording studio called Paisley Park.

TELLING STORIES

The image many non-Minnesotans have of life in the Midwest comes from listening to *A Prairie Home Companion*, a weekly radio show hosted by Garrison Keillor. Each week, Keillor tells stories about a small town he invented called Lake Wobegon. He begins, "It's been a quiet week in Lake Wobegon," and then goes on to spin warm yarns about mild-mannered, eccentric characters whose humble lives somehow always seem to be full of surprises.

Keillor, who was born in Anoka, was a shy boy who read constantly. A high-school English teacher, Deloyd Hockstetter, remembers, "He never contributed to class discussions, but one time he gave a laid-back satire about what's in the records in the principal's office. He had them rolling in the aisles, but everything was written out—that's how shy he was."

In college, Keillor learned to express himself freely on his college radio show. After graduating, he worked at a local radio station, where his warm voice, gentle humor, and hilarious commercials for fake sponsors drew a cult following. In 1974, Keillor began a weekly musical variety show that was broadcast all over the state. The show now plays on hundreds of public radio stations

During his weekly radio program, A Prairie Home Companion, *Garrison Keillor tells stories about a fictional town called Lake Wobegon, Minnesota, "where all the women are strong, all the men are good-looking, and all the children are above average."*

throughout the nation. Keillor is also a successful author, having published such best-selling books as *Lake Wobegon Days* and *Wobegon Boy*.

Though Keillor pokes fun at small-town life, he does it fondly. Critic D. Keith Mano once wrote, "He is in love with the upper Midwest, with the region and the people that Sinclair Lewis derided." If you tune in to his radio show, you may fall in love with Minnesota, too.

Another view of Minnesota was presented in Joel and Ethan Coen's hit film *Fargo*. Growing up in Saint Louis Park, a suburb of

Minneapolis, the brothers were obsessed with movies and even made their own. One early effort, *Lumberjacks of the North*, featured plaid-shirted lumberjacks preparing lunch by pulling pancakes dripping with syrup out of their pockets. As adults, they make devilishly clever movies that they write, produce, and direct themselves.

After a series of brilliant, bizarre films such as *Blood Simple* and *Raising Arizona*, in 1996 the Coens released *Fargo*, an homage to their home state. In the film, a sensible and very pregnant police

Joel and Ethan Coen make quirky movies that are different from anyone else's. Their films have won awards for screenwriting, acting, and directing.

chief, Marge Gunderson, patiently tracks down some bumbling, violent criminals, never losing her calm or her "Minnesota nice." Though *Fargo* pokes fun at the way Minnesotans talk and behave, Marge was the most likable character the Coens had ever created. The film's delightful dialogue earned the Coens an Academy Award for Best Original Screenplay.

A NEW LEADER

By the 1990s, people of color composed more than one-fifth of the population of Minneapolis. Representative of these changes, in

Sharon Sayles Belton, the first woman and the first African American to become mayor of Minneapolis, gives out dictionaries on the first day of school.

1994 Sharon Sayles Belton became the first African American and the first female mayor of Minneapolis. Sayles Belton grew up in the Twin Cities and attended Macalaster College in St. Paul. As a student she was active in the civil rights movement. She later worked as a parole officer before being elected to the Minneapolis City Council.

As mayor, Sayles Belton fought crime by starting a Gang Task Force, increased school funding, promoted youth programs, and encouraged investment in neighborhoods. She was reelected in 1997, serving as an outstanding role model in a city where two-thirds of the public schoolchildren are nonwhite.

6 DIVING IN

If your tour of Minnesota started with an airplane ride to the Twin Cities, your first view of the state might be a wide, flat stretch of farmland that looks like a patchwork quilt. Out of the fields would finally appear an expanse of houses with several lakes nestled among them, and a winding river leading to a cluster of tall, glimmering buildings.

THE TWIN CITIES

You would land at an airport right next to Fort Snelling. The old stone fort has been restored to look just the way it did in 1827. Visitors can watch a blacksmith at work and talk to guides dressed as a surgeon or a trader's wife. Soldiers in 1820s uniforms fire muskets, and the shop sells the kind of candy people ate in frontier days. Nearby, sheltered by the steep, rocky banks of the Minnesota River, is a peaceful park where hikers and cross-country skiers share miles of trails with white-tailed deer and other wildlife.

If you enjoy walking through the lush forests on the riverbanks, check out historic Minnehaha Falls in Minneapolis. *Minnehaha* means "laughing water" (it's easy to remember because of the *haha*). The nearby John H. Stevens House Museum, built in 1849, was the first house in Minneapolis. In it, Minneapolis was named, its government and school districts were organized, its streets were

Musicians entertain visitors at historic Fort Snelling.

mapped, and important meetings with the Dakota Indians were
held. One day in 1896, Minneapolis schools closed so that more
than seven thousand schoolchildren could help move the house to
Minnehaha Park. The children took turns pulling the house on its
six-mile journey.

The Minneapolis Institute of Arts, featuring artwork from around the world, shares a building with the dazzling Children's Theatre. Minneapolis's Walker Art Center specializes in modern art. Its collection features, for example, a twenty-foot bag of french fries. Outside, you can stroll through a garden filled with more than forty sculptures, including one of a gigantic cherry perched on the end

Trees sparkle with newfallen snow near Minnehaha Falls.

The dazzling Frederick R. Weisman Art Museum was described by author M. D. Lake as "an ornament, a fantasy castle that had fallen from the Christmas tree and landed in the snow."

of a spoon. Even more modern is the whimsical Frederick R. Weisman Art Museum at the University of Minnesota, which looks like a shiny tinfoil toy from the outside.

St. Paul's Como Park contains a small zoo and a sparkling glass conservatory filled year-round with lush plants and flowers. Also in St. Paul is a terrific children's museum where you can climb through a maze of tunnels, deliver a television newscast, or operate the controls of a large crane.

The Mall of America in the suburb of Bloomington draws more

visitors than anywhere else in the state. Why would 40 million people a year want to see a mall? For starters, with more than five hundred stores, it's the biggest mall in the entire country. It's so big there are trees inside. Nestled among the trees is a seven-acre amusement park with seventeen rides, including a roller coaster that zooms over the branches. On Saturday nights, so many people fill the mall that it would rank as the third-biggest city in the state.

Wherever you go in the Twin Cities, you won't be far from a river or lake. In summer, you can go swimming or canoeing, or watch a band playing in a lakeside park, the music wafting out across the water. In winter, you can go ice-skating on a frozen lake, then head downtown to warm up. Stores in the Twin Cities are connected by glass "skyways" that allow people to walk from building to building without ever going outside. This can make a big difference when the temperature is below zero. Minneapolis and St. Paul each have five miles of these elevated public walkways—more than any other city in the world.

ON THE ROAD

When you've had your fill of big-city life, it's time to hit the road. One of the first towns you'll see if you drive south is Northfield, where the notorious gang of bank robbers led by Jesse James finally met their match. The Northfield bank that the gang tried to rob is now a museum, with guides that explain exactly how everything happened.

Just south of Northfield is Nerstrand Big Woods State Park.

JESSE JAMES INVADES NORTHFIELD

In 1876, Jesse James and his gang headed north from their base in Missouri to rob the First National Bank in quiet Northfield. The Minnesota townsfolk turned out to be a lot tougher than the gang expected. To their amazement, Joseph Lee Heywood, a substitute cashier, refused to unlock the vault—even with a gun to his head. The gang killed him without getting any money. Another bank employee was shot in the shoulder as he ran away, but by that time the alarm was out. Local businessmen grabbed their guns and fired on the robbers. Two members of the gang were shot dead in the street. The rest fled. Dozens of angry farmers and businessmen joined posses that hunted down the fleeing robbers. Only Frank and Jesse James escaped; Cole, Jim, and Bob Younger were all caught, ending the James-Younger gang forever. The citizens of Northfield are so proud of putting an end to the murderous James-Younger gang that they reenact the event each year in the Defeat of Jesse James Days Festival, which draws 100,000 people.

Jesse James (left) and Frank James

Protected since 1945, this forest is one of the last remaining patches of the Big Woods that once covered several states. Laura Ingalls Wilder described life among the towering hardwoods in *Little House in the Big Woods*, her first book about her pioneer childhood. From the Wisconsin forest, Laura moved to Minnesota, which she described in *On the Banks of Plum Creek*. Fans of the "Little House" books can visit her former home in Walnut Grove, Minnesota. For a taste of pioneer life, visitors can spend a night nearby in an actual sod house, made of chunks of earth.

The rushing streams and rocky river bluffs of Minnesota's southeast corner make it a particularly scenic region. The beautiful river town of Wabasha contains the state's oldest hotel still in use. The Anderson House Hotel has been accepting guests since 1856; today, the hotel lets you choose a cat to take to your room with you.

North of Wabasha, the Mississippi widens to form Lake Pepin, an expanse of water nearly thirty miles long and three miles wide. It's a great place for fishing, sailing, motorboating, and waterskiing. In fact, waterskiing was invented here in 1922, when eighteen-year-old Ralph Samuelson strapped some wooden skis on his feet to see what would happen when he dragged himself behind a boat. Apparently he enjoyed himself, because people have been doing it ever since. Farther south, a fascinating site is Niagara Cave, which contains a sixty-foot-high underground waterfall.

ON THE PRAIRIE

Farther west, the hills end and the earth becomes flat. It's mostly farms now, but it's not hard to imagine what the prairie was like

PLACES TO SEE

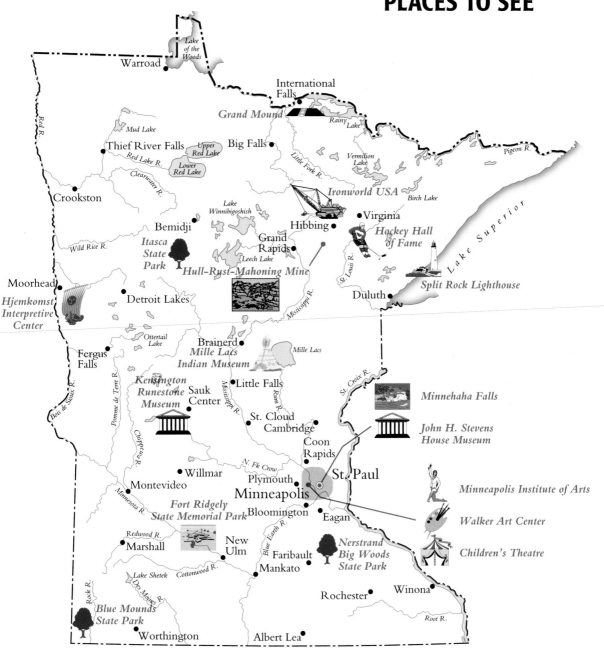

Lake of the Woods

Warroad

International Falls

Grand Mound

Rainy Lake

Red R.

Mud Lake

Thief River Falls

Big Falls

Upper Red Lake

Lower Red Lake

Red Lake R.

Clearwater R.

Little Fork R.

Vermilion Lake

Pigeon R.

Crookston

Lake Winnibigoshish

Ironworld USA

Birch Lake

Bemidji

Virginia

Hockey Hall of Fame

Itasca State Park

Grand Rapids

Hibbing

Leech Lake

Hull-Rust-Mahoning Mine

Lake Superior

Wild Rice R.

St. Louis R.

Split Rock Lighthouse

Moorhead

Hjemkomst Interpretive Center

Detroit Lakes

Duluth

Mississippi R.

Ottertail Lake

Brainerd

Mille Lacs Indian Museum

Mille Lacs

Fergus Falls

Bois de Sioux R.

Pomme de Terre R.

Kensington Runestone Museum

Sauk Center

Little Falls

Mississippi R.

Rum R.

St. Croix R.

Minnehaha Falls

St. Cloud

Cambridge

John H. Stevens House Museum

Chippewa R.

Coon Rapids

Willmar

N. Fk. Crow

St. Paul

Minneapolis Institute of Arts

Montevideo

Plymouth

Minneapolis

Walker Art Center

Minnesota R.

Fort Ridgely State Memorial Park

Bloomington

Eagan

Children's Theatre

Redwood R.

New Ulm

Blue Earth R.

Marshall

Faribault

Nerstrand Big Woods State Park

Lake Shetek

Cottonwood R.

Mankato

Des Moines R.

Rock R.

Blue Mounds State Park

Rochester

Winona

Worthington

Albert Lea

Root R.

Visitors at the Jeffers Petroglyphs in south-western Minnesota can run their hands over pictures that were carved into the rock thousands of years ago.

when the Dakota roamed the land, hunting buffalo. At the Jeffers Petroglyphs, rocks poking up out of the prairie bear almost two thousand pictures, some as much as five thousand years old, carved by Native Americans. Various carvings depict bison, turtles, wolves, bows and arrows, and people.

At Pipestone National Monument, near the western edge of Minnesota, American Indians have been mining the soft, red stone for hundreds of years. This spot is one of the most important places

THE LEGEND OF PIPESTONE

Smoking tobacco originated with the North American Indians. For them, smoking was a sacred act that connected them to the spirit world. This story tells how the Great Spirit brought the Indians the first pipe.

Long ago, the Great Spirit gathered all the different tribes beneath a red ridge of rock. Standing on the edge, he broke a piece from the wall and kneaded it in his hands to form a huge pipe. Then he smoked the pipe, sending smoke out over all the people gathered there. He told them that the stone was their flesh, and that they should make pipes from it. All the tribes were to share this place, and no weapons were ever to be used there. The Great Spirit talked until he had finished smoking, then dissolved into a cloud of smoke. From then on, when the people smoked their sacred pipes at important ceremonies, bringing the smoke into their bodies and then watching it float up into the sky, they felt closer to the spirits who received their offering.

in Native American culture, because only stone dug from this quarry is used to make sacred peace pipes. In the mid-1800s, painter George Catlin visited forty tribes spread over thousands of miles and never saw a pipe that was not made from this stone. Today, Indians still dig up the red pipestone and carve it into pipes and jewelry.

Blue Mounds State Park includes a sharp cliff that appears seemingly out of nowhere. Indians once hunted buffalo by driving them over the edge. A small herd of buffalo lives in the park today. With miles of trails meandering through more than two thousand acres, the park is a good place to explore the prairie.

CENTRAL LAKES

Farther north is Minnesota's central lake country. The popular tourist towns of Brainerd and Detroit Lakes each have more than four hundred lakes within twenty-five miles. In addition to its hundreds of nearby lakes, Alexandria contains the Kensington Runestone Museum, which displays a 202-pound rock covered with carvings. Some believe this runestone was left by Vikings who traveled from Norway in 1362. Norwegians probably did not come that early, but many arrived later, and at the Heritage *Hjemkomst* Interpretive Center in Moorhead you can learn about the region's Scandinavian immigrants. The museum houses a seventy-six-foot replica of a Viking ship named the *Hjemkomst*, which actually sailed to Norway.

Sprawling Mille Lacs Lake in central Minnesota hosts thousands of vacationers in summer and ice-fishers in winter. The excellent

This rocky outcropping in Blue Mounds State Park in southwestern Minnesota is a rare interruption in a sea of flat grassland.

SAILING HOME

Hundreds of years ago, mighty Viking ships sailed from Norway across the Atlantic Ocean. Some say they came all the way to Minnesota by way of the Great Lakes. Robert Asp, a Norwegian-American junior high school teacher in Moorhead, was fascinated by the Vikings. In 1971, he decided to build a Viking ship and sail it back to Norway.

For nine years, Asp and his friends worked on the ship in an old potato warehouse in nearby Hawley. In 1980, the ship was done. It looked just like a real Viking ship made a thousand years ago. Asp named it the *Hjemkomst*, which means "homecoming" in Norwegian.

Asp died later that year. But in 1982, his children launched the beautiful, seventy-six-foot boat from Duluth and sailed across Lake Superior, down the St. Lawrence Seaway, and out into the Atlantic. It was a rough voyage. During one harsh storm, the hull cracked and "the waves just jumped in the boat with us," a crewmember recalled. But the ship made it to Bergen, Norway, where Robert Asp's ancestors had lived. Today, the *Hjemkomst* is on display in a museum in Moorhead.

Tales about the giant lumberjack Paul Bunyan and Babe the Blue Ox flourished among the tall trees and logging camps of northern Minnesota. Several statues of the legendary logger loom over towns such as Bemidji.

Mille Lacs Indian Museum offers exhibits showing how the Ojibwe hunted, fished, collected maple sap, and gathered wild rice two hundred years ago, as well as displays about contemporary Ojibwe life.

If you visit the source of the Mississippi River at Itasca State Park, you can wade across the mighty river where it begins as a twenty-foot-wide stream. Thirty miles northeast is Bemidji, best known

TEN LARGEST CITIES

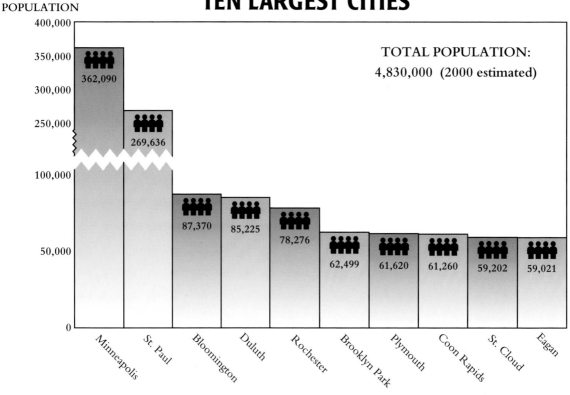

POPULATION

400,000

350,000

300,000

250,000

100,000

50,000

0

TOTAL POPULATION:
4,830,000 (2000 estimated)

362,090 — Minneapolis
269,636 — St. Paul
87,370 — Bloomington
85,225 — Duluth
78,276 — Rochester
62,499 — Brooklyn Park
61,620 — Plymouth
61,260 — Coon Rapids
59,202 — St. Cloud
59,021 — Eagan

for its roadside statues of the legendary lumberjack Paul Bunyan and Babe the Blue Ox. Other towns also feature statues of Paul Bunyan—Brainerd's even talks—but Bemidji's is the oldest, erected in 1937.

UP NORTH

The Iron Range in northeastern Minnesota offers several places to see where the giant mines turned hills and forests into gaping canyons. The Hull-Rust-Mahoning, near Hibbing, is three miles long and two miles wide. According to one visitor, "It looks like a reddish, rusty Grand Canyon." At Ironworld Discovery Center, in Chisholm, a museum shows how the ore was dug and tells the story of the immigrants who worked there. Trolleys take visitors around a once bustling mine site.

In north-central Minnesota, the lakes peter out, and bogs and marshes become plentiful. This region is inhabited mostly by

The mammoth Hull-Rust-Mahoning Mine near Hibbing created a vast canyon that is now a tourist attraction. Over the past hundred years, the mine has yielded hundreds of millions of tons of iron ore.

insects. Koochiching County is so empty that as recently as the 1990s it offered free land to anyone willing to move there. At the northern tip of the state is the immense Lake of the Woods. Ninety miles long, it contains 14,000 islands and endless spots for fishing and ice-fishing.

The Arrowhead region of northeastern Minnesota is filled with thousands of lovely lakes that make it one of the nation's best canoeing areas. For a classic Minnesota vacation, do what many Twin Cities residents do: hop in the car and head north on Interstate 35. Before long, the buildings thin out and you're surrounded by farms. You'll pass a few lakes and start seeing more and more trees, but for the most part it's a quiet, relaxing drive through fields of corn and alfalfa. After about three hours, you climb to the top of a large hill. Spread out below is the city of Duluth, wrapped around a shimmering harbor at the tip of Lake Superior.

Past Duluth, a road follows the lakeshore eastward. You're in the woods now, and you keep catching glimpses of glistening water through the trees. It's suddenly much cooler than it was in the Twin Cities. At times the road rises and hugs a rocky cliff, and the view of the cool blue water is breathtaking. Frothing rivers cut through the rocks to splash into Lake Superior, the largest freshwater lake in the world. The long, sleepy drive has made you restless; you can't wait to get out and run among the rocks and trees, picking wild raspberries along the lake's rugged, rocky north shore.

If you drive even farther north, into the woods, you will soon be gliding your canoe across the rippling water of a crystal-clear lake. Quite likely you'll see a loon bobbing near you. As Chester Anderson

The worn, weathered rocks on the north shore of Lake Superior are a great place for kids to play.

wrote in *Growing Up in Minnesota*, "It's worth the trip, especially for kids, to hear the loony laughter. First the loon laughs. A kid will laugh back, naturally, and the loon will reply, joining in an endless exchange of echoing fun. Minnesota is a good place in which to grow up."

THE FLAG: The state flag is deep blue with a gold fringe. In the center is the state seal surrounded by a wreath of lady's slippers, the state flower. Around the wreath is a ring of 19 stars, representing the fact that Minnesota was the 19th state admitted to the Union after the 13 original states. The flag was adopted in 1957.

THE SEAL: The state seal, adopted in 1861, shows a farmer plowing a field by hand near a waterfall on the Mississippi River. His ax, gun, and powder horn rest on a nearby stump, and he is watching an Indian on horseback riding by. Above the farmer and Indian is a scroll with the state motto in French, L'Etoile du Nord. Surrounding this scene is a border that reads "The Great Seal of the State of Minnesota, 1858."

STATE SURVEY

Statehood: May 11, 1858

Origin of Name: From a Dakota Indian term for "sky-tinted water"

Nickname: Gopher State, Land of 10,000 Lakes

Capital: St. Paul

Motto: The Star of the North

Bird: Common loon

Fish: Walleye

Flower: Pink and white lady's slippers

Tree: Norway pine

Gem: Lake Superior agate

Walleye

Pink and white lady's slipper

HAIL! MINNESOTA

Truman Rickard, who graduated from the University of Minnesota in 1904, wrote the music and this verse of "Hail! Minnesota," which was the school song until it was adopted as the official state song in 1945.

By Truman E. Rickard

Min-ne-so-ta, hail to thee! Hail to thee, our col-lege dear!__ Thy__

light shall ev-er be A__ bea-con bright and clear. Thy__

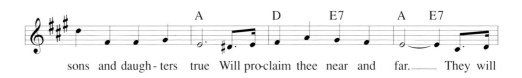

sons and daugh-ters true Will pro-claim thee near and far.__ They will

guard thy fame and a-dore thy name; Thou shalt be their North-ern Star.

Beverage: Milk

Grain: Wild rice

Mushroom: Morel

GEOGRAPHY

Highest Point: 2,301 feet above sea level, at Eagle Mountain in Cook County

Lowest Point: 602 feet, along Lake Superior

Area: 86,943 square miles

Greatest Distance, North to South: 411 miles

Greatest Distance, East to West: 357 miles

Bordering States: Wisconsin to the east, Iowa to the south, North Dakota and South Dakota to the west, and the Canadian provinces of Manitoba and Ontario to the north

Hottest Recorded Temperature: 114°F at Beardsley on July 29, 1917, and at Moorhead on July 6, 1936

Coldest Recorded Temperature: -60°F at Tower on February 2, 1996

Average Annual Precipitation: 26 inches

Major Rivers: Blue Earth, Cannon, Crow Wing, Little Fork, Middle, Minnesota, Mississippi, Pomme de Terre, Rapid, Red, Red Lake, Redwood, St. Croix, St. Louis, Thief, Wild Rice

Major Lakes: Big Sandy, Bowstring, Kabetogama, Lake of the Woods, Leech, Lower Red, Mille Lacs, Minnetonka, Minnewaska, Osakis, Otter

Tail, Pelican, Pepin, Pokegama, Superior, Upper Red, Vermilion, Winnibigoshish

Trees: ash, aspen, balsam, beech, birch, black walnut, elm, fir, maple, oak, pine, poplar, spruce

Wild Plants: aster, bird's-foot violet, blazing star, bulrush, goldenrod, honeysuckle, lady's slipper, prairie phlox, sweet fern, thimbleberry, trailing arbutus, water lily, wintergreen

Animals: badger, beaver, black bear, bobcat, fox, gopher, moose, opossum, otter, porcupine, raccoon, skunk, squirrel, white-tailed deer

Birds: bald eagle, blackbird, duck, loon, meadowlark, owl, pheasant, sparrow, woodpecker, wren

Fish: bass, carp, catfish, lake herring, muskellunge, northern pike, smelt, trout, walleye, whitefish, yellow perch

Endangered Animals: Baird's sparrow, Blanding's turtle, burrowing owl, chestnut-collared longspur, gray wolf, Henslow's sparrow, northern cricket frog, peregrine falcon, piping plover, Sprague's pipit, Uhler's arctic butterfly, wood turtle

Burrowing owl

Endangered Plants: bog adder's mouth, dwarf trout lily, Indian ricegrass, kitten-tails, knotty pearlwort, nodding saxifrage, Norwegian draba, purple crowberry, rams-head lady's slipper, wolf's spike rush

TIMELINE

Minnesota History

1600s Ojibwe Indians migrate to northern Minnesota from Canada

1660 French traders Pierre Radisson and Médard Chouart explore the Minnesota shores of Lake Superior

1679 Daniel Greysolon, Sieur Du Luth, explores northeastern Minnesota and claims the region for France

1680 Father Louis Hennepin discovers the Falls of St. Anthony on the site of present-day Minneapolis

1689 The French build a trading post named St. Antoine, the first in the region, near Lake Pepin

1732 Pierre Gautier de Varennes, Sieur de La Vérendryes, builds the first French fort in Minnesota on the shores of the Lake of the Woods

1762 France cedes land in Minnesota west of the Mississippi River to Spain

1763 France cedes land in Minnesota east of the Mississippi River to England as part of the treaty ending the French and Indian War

1783 The United States gains the part of Minnesota east of the Mississippi as a result of its victory in the American Revolution

1803 The United States gains the rest of Minnesota as part of the Louisiana Purchase

1820 Construction begins on Fort St. Anthony at the site where the Mississippi and Minnesota Rivers join; it is renamed Fort Snelling in 1825

1832 Henry Schoolcraft discovers the source of the Mississippi River at Lake Itasca in north-central Minnesota

1837 Dakota and Ojibwe Indians cede a large portion of their territory in east-central Minnesota to the United States

1849 The Minnesota Territory is created

1851 Dakota Indians sign a treaty giving up their remaining territory in southern Minnesota

1858 Minnesota becomes the 32nd state

1862 Dakota Indians, angry at land treaties and U.S. Indian policies, launch an uprising that kills hundreds

1889 The physician William Mayo and his sons begin operating a hospital in Rochester

1892 The first shipments of iron ore leave the Mesabi Range

1918 Forest fires destroy about 2,000 square miles of forest in northeastern Minnesota and kill hundreds of people

1930 Floyd Olson of the Farmer-Labor Party is elected governor, the first person from a third party elected to the governership of any state

1944 The Farmer-Labor Party merges with the Democratic Party, giving the Democrats strong support among rural Minnesotans

1959 The opening of the St. Lawrence Seaway makes Duluth the westernmost port connected to the Atlantic Ocean

1969 Minnesotan Warren Burger is appointed chief justice of the U.S. Supreme Court

1992 The state pioneers a health-insurance program to help the poor and unemployed

1993 Almost half of Minnesota's counties are declared disaster areas because of severe flooding of the Mississippi River

1994 Sharon Sayles Belton becomes the first African-American mayor of Minneapolis

ECONOMY

Agricultural Products: beef, butter, cheese, corn, milk, pork, potatoes, poultry, rye, soybeans, sugar beets, wheat

Corn harvest

Manufactured Products: canned foods, cereals, chemicals, computers and computer equipment, farm and construction machinery, paper products, printed materials, scientific and medical instruments

Natural Resources: granite, gravel, iron ore, limestone, lumber, sandstone, taconite

Business and Trade: banking, communications, data processing, health care, insurance, transportation, wholesale and retail sales

CALENDAR OF CELEBRATIONS

Burns Night Each January 24, the town of Mapleton joins people of Scottish descent throughout the world in celebrating the birthday of the Scottish poet Robert Burns. The celebration includes Scottish song and dance, bagpipe music, and traditional Scottish foods.

Cabin Fever Days At the end of January the people of Cannon Falls treat their winter "cabin fever" with a celebration featuring sled-dog races, ski races, and a parade of horse-drawn sleighs.

St. Paul Winter Carnival More than 100 years old, this weeklong festival in late January and early February is the nation's oldest and largest winter festival. It features more than 100 events, including parades, cultural celebrations, and ice- and snow-sculpting competitions.

Ice Box Days International Falls celebrates its famously frigid winters each January with various winter events. Included are the Freeze Yer Gizzard Blizzard 10k race and the Frostbite Falls Ski Classic. Visitors are advised to bring plenty of warm clothes.

Fasching Held on the day before the beginning of Lent (usually in

February), the Fasching at New Ulm is the traditional German equivalent of Mardi Gras. The festival includes music, costume contests, German food, and arts and crafts.

St. Urho's Day Each March the town of Finland holds a celebration in honor of a Finnish saint who supposedly drove the grasshoppers out of Finland. The celebration includes a parade, music, dancing, and food.

Annual Eagle Watch Bird-watchers from around the United States gather in Stillwater each March to view the annual migration of bald eagles along the St. Croix River.

Mai Feiertag In May the town of Montrose celebrates spring and its German heritage with a traditional German celebration featuring music and dancing. It also includes a maypole raising—the erecting of a tall pole festooned with ribbons, which people dance around to celebrate spring.

Eagle Creek Rendezvous Held in May in the town of Shakopee, this event recreates the fur-trading gatherings of the 1800s. There are tepees, tomahawk throwing demonstrations, music, and other activities.

Ripplin' River Daze Held in Zumbro Falls in June, this festival features parades, sports competitions, street dancing, fireworks, an exhibit of artifacts showcasing the town's history in the 1890s, and lots of food.

Great American Think-Off Each June, New York Mills hosts this national philosophy competition geared toward the everyday person rather than academic scholars. Finalists participate in a live philosophical debate, and the audience chooses the winner.

Vikingland Band Festival The finest high school marching bands in the Midwest gather in Alexandria each June to stage a dazzling parade competition. This event typically draws over 2,000 performers and more than 30,000 spectators.

Timber Days In June the town of Cook celebrates its lumber industry with a festival featuring lumberjack contests, craft demonstrations, art, food, and entertainment. Also included are a carnival and parade.

Bean Hole Days The people of Pequot Lakes cook 150 gallons of Boston baked beans in the ground each July in honor of the New England origin of the town's name. The event also features other foods and an arts-and-crafts fair.

Wrong Days In July the town of Wright celebrates its opposite—wrong—with dances, amateur talent contests, a crafts fair, sports competitions, a parade, and a smorgasbord of good food.

Upper Sioux Wacipi The Dakota Sioux Indian ceremony wacipi honors tribal elders, youth, and departed loved ones. Held in July at the Upper Sioux Agency State Park, it includes ceremonial dress, drumming, and singing.

Finnish Festival Each August Chisholm honors the Finnish immigrants who came to the region with a celebration featuring ethnic dances, authentic costumes, crafts, and spectacular musical productions.

Stiftungsfest This festival of singing, dancing, sports contests, food, and rides originated in 1861, making it the oldest festival in Minnesota. It is held in August between the towns of Norwood and Young America.

Summer contest on the lake

Itasca Pioneer Farmers Show Held at Lake Itasca in August, this event features parades, old-time tractor pulls, lumber-sawing contests, demonstrations of farm activities, logging displays, and traditional music.

Minnesota State Fair Held annually in St. Paul around the end of August and beginning of September, this is one of the nation's largest and best-attended agricultural fairs. More than 1 million visitors come to see exhibits of fine arts, baked goods, crafts, and much more. The livestock competitions are a favorite.

Mill City Music Festival This event, held each September in Minneapolis, is one of the largest music festivals in the Midwest. It showcases nationally renowned musicians and also celebrates regional and local music. Visitors to the festival can hear all types of music, ranging from blues and jazz to rock, gospel, and ethnic music.

Festival of Lights Between the end of November and beginning of January, Canal Park in Duluth lights up the holiday season with Christmas parades, special events, and colorful holiday displays.

STATE STARS

Charles Bender (1883–1954), a member of the Baseball Hall of Fame, was born on the White Earth Indian Reservation near Brainerd. The son of a German-American father and Ojibwe mother, Bender played baseball and football at the Carlisle Indian School in Pennsylvania. He signed with the Philadelphia Athletics in 1903 and played in several World Series. In 1913 he became the first pitcher to win six World Series games. After retiring he worked as a college and major league coach.

Patty Berg (1913–　), one of the greatest female golfers ever, was born in Minneapolis. Berg began playing amateur golf in her teens and gained national recognition by age 17. She turned professional in 1940 and won more than 80 tournaments, including a record 15 major championships. A founder of the U.S. Ladies' Professional Golfers' Association, Berg also served as its first president. She was elected to the Golfing Hall of Fame in 1974.

Patty Berg

Harry A. Blackmun (1908–　) was an associate justice of the U.S. Supreme Court. Although born in Illinois, Blackmun grew up in Minneapolis and St. Paul. After earning a law degree at Harvard in 1932, he returned to Minnesota to practice law. In 1959 he was appointed to the U.S. Court of Appeals. He was appointed to the U.S. Supreme Court in 1970. In 1973 Blackmun wrote the majority opinion in *Roe v. Wade*, the landmark decision that gave women the right to choose to have abortions. Blackmun retired from the Court in 1994.

Robert Bly (1926–　), a poet and lecturer, was born in Madison. After serving in the navy in World War II, Bly studied literature and earned a degree from Harvard University in 1950. He has spent his life writing, lecturing, and teaching. In the 1960s he became a well-known activist protesting the Vietnam War. In 1990 Bly published a book called *Iron John: A Book about Men*, which became a best-seller and helped launch a movement among men to rediscover their masculinity.

Warren E. Burger (1907–1995), a chief justice of the U.S. Supreme Court, was born in St. Paul. Burger began practicing law in 1931 and became involved in the civil rights struggle in the 1940s. In 1953 he was appointed assistant attorney general in charge of civil rights. He was named chief justice of the Supreme Court in 1969. On the Court, Burger worked hard to improve the efficiency of the entire judicial system. He retired in 1986.

Warren E. Burger

William O. Douglas (1898–1980), born in Maine, Minnesota, served as an associate justice of the U.S. Supreme Court from 1939 to 1975—the longest any individual has served on the Court. After graduating from Columbia University Law School in 1925, Douglas worked briefly as a corporate lawyer and then taught law. In 1939 President Franklin Roosevelt appointed him to the U.S. Supreme Court. Only 40 years old at the time, Douglas was the second-youngest justice in the Court's history. During his many years on the Court, Douglas became known for his outspoken defense of civil liberties, especially freedom of speech and the press.

Richard G. Eberhart (1904–   ), a well-known poet, was born in Austin. The author of several respected collections of poetry, including *A Bravery of Earth* and *Burr Oaks*, Eberhart has also taught literature at several colleges, including the University of Washington and Dartmouth College. Eberhart has won a number of prestigious awards, including the Pulitzer

Prize in 1966. Many of his poems reflect a love for nature that he gained as a young boy living in rural Minnesota.

Richard G. Eberhart

Judy Garland (1922–1969), a popular singer and actress, was born Frances Gumm in Grand Rapids. The daughter of entertainers, Garland first appeared onstage at age three. She later toured the United States with her sisters in a musical act. Garland made her first film in 1936 and soon became a well-known child star. Her role as Dorothy in *The Wizard of Oz* made her one of the most famous stars in Hollywood.

Judy Garland

J. Paul Getty (1892–1976), born in Minneapolis, was reportedly the wealthiest man in the world at the time of his death. Getty began buying and selling oil leases in Oklahoma in 1913 with the help of his father, an oil millionaire. A gifted entrepreneur, the younger Getty earned his first million by age 24. During the 1920s he gained control of several oil companies and built a financial empire. He was a billionaire by the mid-1950s. The J. Paul Getty Museum in California, founded by Getty in 1953, displays many of the art objects he collected during his lifetime.

Hubert H. Humphrey (1911–1978), a vice president of the United States, was born in Wallace, South Dakota, but spent much of his adult life in Minnesota. Humphrey became involved in politics in 1944, when he served as the Minnesota campaign manager for President Franklin Roosevelt. He launched his own political career in 1945, when he was elected mayor of Minneapolis. In 1948 Humphrey was elected to the U.S. Senate. He served there for 16 years, gaining a reputation as an effective leader and strong supporter of liberal ideas. Elected vice president under Lyndon Johnson in 1964, Humphrey worked on civil rights and antipoverty programs. He ran for president in 1968 but was narrowly defeated by Richard Nixon.

Jessica Lange (1949–   ), an award-winning actress, was born in Cloquet. She first pursued a career in art and then began studying acting while living in New York. Her first movie was a remake of the classic *King Kong*. Lange went on to become one of the most respected actresses in Hollywood. She won the Oscar for Best Supporting Actress in 1982 for her role in *Tootsie* and the Oscar for Best Actress in 1994 for her performance in *Blue Sky*. In recent years, Lange has returned to live in Minnesota.

Jessica Lange

Charles Lindbergh (1902–1974), a famous aviator, was born in Detroit, Michigan, but spent his childhood in Little Falls. Lindbergh learned to fly at age 20 and started flying a mail route between Chicago and St. Louis in 1926. In 1927, in a plane called the *Spirit of St. Louis*, he became the first person to fly solo across the Atlantic Ocean. The successful flight made Lindbergh a worldwide hero. Tragedy struck Lindbergh and his wife in 1932 when their infant son was kidnapped and murdered.

Charles Lindbergh

John Madden (1936–   ), a sports commentator and former football coach, was born in Austin. Involved in sports throughout his school years, Madden was drafted by the Philadelphia Eagles in 1959, but a leg injury ended his professional career before it even began. Unable to play, he turned to coaching. He coached the Oakland Raiders for 10 years, leading them to a Super Bowl championship in 1977. In 1979 Madden began teaching, acting in commercials, and broadcasting sports commentaries on radio and television. He has won several Emmy Awards as a sports analyst and commentator.

Roger Maris (1934–1985), a baseball outfielder, was born in Hibbing. Maris played football and baseball in high school and began playing minor league baseball in 1953. In 1957 he entered the major leagues, playing for the Cleveland Indians, Kansas City Athletics, and New York Yankees.

Roger Maris

In 1961, while with the Yankees, Maris made baseball history by hitting 61 home runs in a single season, a record that stood until 1998.

Eugene McCarthy (1916–   ), a U.S. senator and presidential candidate, was born in Watkins. After serving in World War II, McCarthy taught college. He ran successfully for the U.S. House of Representatives in 1948 and served until 1958, when he was elected to the Senate. An outspoken critic of the Vietnam War, McCarthy challenged President Lyndon Johnson in Democratic primaries for the 1968 presidential election. Although unsuccessful, he continued to speak out against the war. McCarthy retired from the Senate in 1970.

Walter Mondale (1928–   ), a vice president of the United States, was born in Ceylon. Trained as a lawyer, he became active in politics in college when he worked on Hubert Humphrey's first campaign for the U.S. Senate. In 1965 Mondale was appointed to Humphrey's seat when the senator became vice president. Elected to the Senate on his own in 1966, he won reelection in 1972. In 1976 he ran successfully for vice president under President Jimmy Carter. While in office, Mondale favored liberal policies and was a strong supporter of civil rights and education reform. In 1984 he ran unsuccessfully for the presidency against Ronald Reagan.

Winona Ryder (1971–   ), a highly respected actress, was born Winona Horowitz and named after her birthplace of Winona, Minnesota. Ryder had an unconventional childhood, moving with her nonconformist, intellectual parents to a communal farm in California when she was about 10. She began taking acting classes at age 13 and found that she loved playing different characters. Noticed by a talent scout, she got her first movie role while she was in the eighth grade. Ryder has appeared in many movies, including *The Age of Innocence* and *The Crucible*.

Winona Ryder

Harrison E. Salisbury (1908–1993), a well-known author and journalist, was born in Minneapolis. Although he planned to be a chemist, he discovered his talent as a journalist while reporting for his college newspaper. Salisbury began working for the United Press in 1930 and moved to the agency's London office in 1943. A few years later he joined the *New York Times* and became a well-known foreign correspondent. Salisbury returned to New York in 1954 and worked as an editor and correspondent for the *Times* for many years, during which he won a number of journalism awards and honors.

Charles Schulz (1922–   ), the cartoonist who created the comic strip *Peanuts* about Charlie Brown, Snoopy, and their friends, was born in Minneapolis. Not a particularly good student, Schulz began drawing cartoons in high school. After serving in World War II, he settled in St. Paul and began drawing a weekly cartoon for a local newspaper. Within a few years *Peanuts* was born, and it soon appeared in newspapers across the country. Schulz has published a number of collections of the comic strip.

Richard W. Sears (1863–1914) was a merchant who founded one of the nation's most successful mail-order businesses. Born in Stewartville, Sears worked for the railroad for a number of years. He began selling watches through the mail in 1886. He soon hired an assistant, Alvah Roebuck, and moved the business to Chicago. The business expanded quickly, and Sears took Roebuck on as a partner. The company eventually became known as Sears, Roebuck and Company. By 1894 the company's mail-order catalog had more than 500 pages of items for sale.

Elaine Stately (1937–1988), a Native American activist, was born on the White Earth Indian Reservation in west-central Minnesota. An Ojibwe Indian, Stately was one of the founders of the American Indian Movement, an Indian civil rights group established in 1972. She also started a Native American Olympics.

DeWitt Wallace (1889–1981), the founder of *Reader's Digest* magazine, was born in St. Paul. After attending college, Wallace worked for several years as a book salesman in St. Paul. While selling books, he got the idea of publishing a magazine that contained articles gathered from other magazines. He brought his idea to life in 1920 when he began publishing

Reader's Digest. Wallace's magazine went on to become one of the most popular in the United States.

Dave Winfield (1951–   ), an all-star baseball player, was born in St. Paul. In high school Winfield excelled in both baseball and basketball, but he focused on baseball in college. He began his professional baseball career in 1973 when he joined the San Diego Padres. He played for the Padres until 1980 and established himself as one of the stars of the team. In 1980 Winfield signed with the New York Yankees for a record-breaking salary of $20 million over 10 years. Winfield later played for the California Angels and the Toronto Blue Jays before ending his career with the Minnesota Twins in 1993.

TOUR THE STATE

Boundary Waters Canoe Area Wilderness (Ely) A unique preserve of forest and water, the Boundary Waters is the greatest wilderness canoeing and fishing area in the world. More than one thousand lakes and streams lie within this vast forested area, offering canoeists remote solitude and unspoiled beauty.

Split Rock Lighthouse (Two Harbors) Located on the shores of Lake Superior, this lighthouse has warned ships away from a dangerous rocky coast since 1910. One of Minnesota's best-known landmarks, it offers a glimpse of life in a remote and spectacular setting. In addition to touring the lighthouse, you can visit a history center that features exhibits and a film.

Split Rock Lighthouse

Fort Snelling (Minneapolis) This restored stone military post was built between 1820 and 1825. It features exhibits of artifacts and demonstrations showing what life was like in Minnesota in the 1820s.

Sibley House (Mendota) Built in 1836, this historic stone building was the home of Henry H. Sibley, a prominent fur trader and Minnesota's first state governor. Exhibits and guided tours reveal information about Sibley and his family, the fur trade, and the history of Native Americans of the region.

Forest History Center (Grand Rapids) A re-creation of a turn-of-the-century logging camp, the center features exhibits, logging demonstrations, forest trails, and lectures about forest resource conservation.

Mall of America (Bloomington) The largest shopping mall in the United States, the enormous Mall of America includes more than 500 stores, 14 movie theaters, dozens of restaurants, and an indoor amusement park complete with a roller coaster.

Mille Lacs Indian Museum (Onamia) Exhibits at this museum trace the history of the Mille Lacs band of Ojibwe Indians. The museum also features craft demonstrations and films about modern Ojibwe life.

Murphy's Landing (Shakopee) This re-creation of an 1890s Minnesota pioneer village features replicas of farms, a fur trader's cabin, a small Native American village, and other period buildings.

Pipestone National Monument (Pipestone) This monument preserves land held sacred to many Native American tribes. The Indians came here because of the soft red stone, which they used to make peace pipes and other objects. An interpretive center tells about the quarry's history and geology and displays Indian crafts.

Charles A. Lindbergh State Park (Little Falls) This park is built around the childhood home of the famous aviator. Built in 1906, the house contains some original Lindbergh family possessions. The park also includes a history center with exhibits on Lindbergh and the area.

Lumbertown USA (Brainerd) This popular attraction contains 26 buildings that recreate a logging town of the 1870s. Among them are a store, a school, and a saloon.

Minnesota History Center (St. Paul) The center houses many exhibits about Minnesota history—everything from a 24-ton boxcar to a canoe used for fur trading. Visitors can watch presentations by costumed characters representing various periods in the state's history.

St. Anthony Falls Historic District (Minneapolis) Visitors to this historic district can view the only waterfall on the Mississippi River, as well as the ruins of a flour-milling district that was once the largest in the world. A self-guided trail running for two miles along the Minneapolis riverfront has signs describing the history of the Native Americans and the early settlers of the riverfront area.

Jeffers Petroglyphs (Jeffers) Amid acres of prairie grasses are islands of rock where ancient Indians made carvings, known as petroglyphs, of people and animals. Some estimated to be 5,000 years old, the carvings record important events and ceremonies. A visitor center and self-guided trails focus on the history of the petroglyphs and the ecological changes that have occurred at the site over the last 5,000 years.

Grand Portage National Monument (Grand Portage) Located at the northeast tip of Minnesota, the monument includes a restored fur trading post originally built by the North West Company. Costumed guides take visitors back to the days of the French fur traders and explorers. Nearby Grand Portage State Park offers scenic views of a spectacular 200-foot waterfall, the highest in Minnesota.

Minnesota Museum of Mining (Chisholm) The museum has a restored iron-mining village and other exhibits that tell the story of mining in the state.

Oliver H. Kelley Farm and Interpretive Center (Elk River) This farm museum was the birthplace of the National Grange, a farm organization founded in 1867 that worked to improve the lives of farmers. The center features actual farm activities and demonstrations of domestic crafts, such as quilting, basket making, and blacksmithing.

Hull-Rust-Mahoning Mine (Hibbing) Known as the Grand Canyon of Minnesota, this is the largest open-pit mine in the world. The enormous iron mine is 3 miles long, 2 miles wide, and 500 feet deep.

Voyageurs National Park (International Falls) Minnesota's only national park, Voyageurs features 30 lakes and a network of interconnected waterways. Originally part of the "water highway" that carried fur traders through the region, the park is very popular for canoeing and camping.

North Shore Commercial Fishing Museum (Tofte) Housed in a replica of a deep red fish house built by early fishermen in the area, the museum features displays on the lives of early settlers and the fishing industry.

International Wolf Center (Ely) This center features exhibits on wolf legends and behavior, hands-on activities and interactive exhibits for kids, and various naturalist programs.

FUN FACTS

Because of its thousands of lakes, Minnesota has more miles of shoreline than California, Florida, and Hawaii combined.

One of the largest log jams in history occurred on the St. Croix River near Taylors Falls in 1886. It took 200 men six weeks to break up the jam, which ran for about two miles along the river.

From its founding in 1838 until 1841, St. Paul was called Pig's Eye, after its first settler, Pierre "Pig's Eye" Parrant.

During the winter of 1888 the people of St. Paul built an ice palace for its winter festival. Until the weather warmed up and melted it, the ice structure was one of the largest buildings in the world—14 stories high and covering an acre of land.

FIND OUT MORE

If you want to learn more about Minnesota, check your local library or bookstore for these titles:

BOOKS

General State Books

Fradin, Dennis Brindell, and Judith Bloom Fradin. *Minnesota*. Danbury, CT: Children's Press, 1997.

Thompson, Kathleen. *Minnesota*. Austin, TX: Raintree, 1996.

Special Interest Books

Berg, Lois Anne. *An Eritrean Family*. Minneapolis: Lerner, 1997.

Carlson, Jeffrey D. *A Historical Album of Minnesota*. Brookfield, CT: Millbrook, 1994.

Mohr, Howard. *How to Talk Minnesotan*. New York: Penguin, 1987.

Moore, David L. *Dark Sky, Dark Land: Stories of the Hmong Boy Scouts of Troop 100*. Eden Prairie, MN: Tessera, 1989.

Murphy, Nora. *A Hmong Family*. Minneapolis: Lerner, 1997.

Tanner, Helen Hornbeck. *The Ojibwa*. New York: Chelsea House, 1991.

Fiction

Marvin, Isabel. *A Bride for Anna's Papa*. Minneapolis: Milkweed, 1994. During the 1907 labor strife on the Iron Range, thirteen-year-old Anna tries to find a new wife for her father after her mother's death.

Thomas, Jane Resh. *Courage at Indian Deep*. New York: Clarion, 1990. A boy must help the survivors of a shipwreck during a blizzard on Lake Superior.

Wilder, Laura Ingalls. *On the Banks of Plum Creek*. New York: HarperTrophy, 1973. A classic about a young girl's life on the frontier.

AUDIOCASSETTES AND CDS

Dylan, Bob. *Biograph*. Sony, 1987.

Keillor, Garrison. *News from Lake Wobegon*. HighBridge, 1992.

VIDEOS

The Dakota Conflict. Garrison Keillor, narrator. Acorn Media, 1995.

WEBSITES

http://www.startribune.com. The Minneapolis Star Tribune website contains newspaper articles on all subjects and links to Minnesota-related websites.

http://www.state.mn.us. Minnesota state government website.

INDEX

Chart, graph, and illustration page numbers are in boldface.